PROCLAIMING
GOD'S
Word

a handbook for readers
MARGARET RIZZA

Kevin
Mayhew

First published in 1995 by the
Archdiocese of Southwark Liturgy Commission

This edition published by
KEVIN MAYHEW LTD
Buxhall
Stowmarket
Suffolk IP14 3BW

1 2 3 4 5 6 7 8 9

ISBN 1 84003 271 5
Catalogue No 1500234

Cover design by Jaquetta Sergeant
Edited by Helen Elliot
Typesetting by Louise Selfe

Printed and bound in Great Britain

Contents _____

Foreword by the Archbishop of Southwark　　　　4

Introduction　　　　5

Chapter 1　　*The Word of All Life*　　　　7

Chapter 2　　*Spiritual Preparation*　　　　13

Chapter 3　　*Practical Preparation*　　　　23

Chapter 4　　*The Lectionary*　　　　32

Chapter 5　　*Putting It into Practice*　　　　35

Chapter 6　　*Conclusion*　　　　40

Appendix 1　　*Commissioning of Parish Readers*　　　　43

Appendix 2　　*Description of the Order of Readings*　　　　47

Appendix 3　　*A Guide to Biblical Pronunciation*　　　　65

Bibliography　　　　78

Acknowledgements　　　　79

Foreword

It is of the greatest importance to have readers who can proclaim the Word of God well. This handbook will help towards achieving that. I would like to thank Margaret Rizza, who is a member of the Liturgical Formation Committee of the Diocesan Commission for the Liturgy, for writing this document and I recommend it to all who are involved in reading in our parishes. It is both informative in the practical advice it gives, and inspiring in reminding people of all that is involved in this special ministry and service in the Church.

✠ Michael Bowen
Archbishop of Southwark
1995

Introduction

This handbook for readers has been culled from the experience of over five years' work of Readers' days, workshops and courses in various parishes in the Diocese of Southwark. Much of this work has been shared with Angela Lawrence from whom I have learnt much and to whom I wish to give grateful thanks for all the support she has given me. I am also indebted to Father John Wijngaards for the rich resources of his writings on the Word which have given me much inspiration.

Many parish readers have expressed a very real need for some sort of guide which would help them to:

- understand more fully the sacred significance, importance and value of this ministry;
- understand something of the technical aspects of how the Proclamation of the Word can be developed;
- deepen their understanding of what it means to prepare and pray over Scripture.

The handbook, written in some depth, is to be dipped into or referred to according to the individual needs of the reader. It is a handbook which, I hope, will help the Word of God to be proclaimed to the assembly as clearly and meaningfully as each reader is able to do in their own unique and individual way.

I have worked closely with the members of the Liturgical Formation Committee of the Diocese of Southwark Commission for the Liturgy and they have given me much help with their comments, suggestions and advice. I wish to extend to them my very sincere thanks. I would like to thank especially Fr Anthony Charlton for all his guidance, patience and encouragement in helping me to produce this little guide. Without him it would not have been written.

Margaret Rizza
September 1998

Chapter 1 _____

_____ *The Word of All Life*

Something which has existed since the beginning,
that we have heard,
that we have seen with our own eyes;
that we have watched
and touched with our hands:
THE WORD, who is life –
this is our subject. (1 John 1:1)

By sharing in this ministry of service to their parish community, the reader enables the Word of God to be proclaimed in the midst of the assembly. Since Vatican II the Word of God has been restored as a living and life-giving event, the Council insisting that God's Word is the source of all life. The task of the Church in our time is to give God's living Word back to the people.

In order to perform our task effectively we need to know something of the nature of the Word, its purpose, and the means of bringing the Word to life. The purpose of proclaiming the living Word of God in the midst of the assembly is to help the members experience the living and life-giving presence of Jesus who is the Word. This experience of the presence of Jesus depends on the members of the assembly consciously and deliberately taking on the role of listener. The community is called to listen. Without listeners there is no living Word. Through genuine listening – listening with the ear of the heart – we open ourselves to the power of the Spirit who heals us, enabling us to grow and transform our lives. The task is clear; we need to form life-giving readers and life-receiving listeners.

Proclamation of the Word is essentially storytelling. Storytelling has the power to bring both teller and listener into the storytelling world, and to transform them through the power of the story. When we proclaim the Word of the Lord we are telling God's story. But God's story is also our story. In the telling and listening we are able to merge into the mystery of God's love, of Jesus' dying and rising. We become profoundly aware of who we are, and where we come from, what we are for and where we are going.

The power of the Word

Scripture comes from God. God is the author and from these writings we learn about the revelation of divine love. In this book, *The Bible*, we are told many things about God; who God is; what God does; what God wants of us. In it there are wonderful writings of love from a Father to his children; from a Mother who loves and longs to protect her errant, exiled family: 'How often have I longed to gather your children, as a hen gathers her brood under her wings!' (Luke 13:34). We are loved so much, so unconditionally that, at a certain moment in history, God sends his beloved Son, Jesus, into our world of time and space to free us, to teach us about his Kingdom, to bring us to fullness of being and to share in his eternal life.

To understand something about the creative power of the Word it is helpful to go back in time to see what the Word signified in the Jewish and Greek traditions.

For the Jewish people the Word was very much more than just a sound. It had an independent energy – a power which enabled things to happen. The Old Testament describes God's Word as creative, energetic, even explosive. By means of his Word God brings the universe into being. Fire and water are two particularly powerful images which the great prophets used to describe the dynamic activity of God's Word. Fire refines and purifies, while water nourishes and gives life.

The prophets Malachi and Jeremiah experience the Word of God as the refiner's fire which burns away all deception, revealing only the truth (see Malachi 3:2-3). In Isaiah we read how the Word is like refreshing water: 'Yes, as the rain and the snow come down from the heavens and do not return without watering the earth, making it yield and giving growth to provide seed for the sower and bread for the eating, so the Word that goes from my mouth does not return to me empty, without carrying out my will and succeeding in what it was sent to do' (Isaiah 55:10-11).

The Jews also had another understanding of the Word. They thought of it in terms of Wisdom. In the Wisdom Books there are certain passages which attribute a mysterious, life-giving and eternal power to Wisdom (Proverbs 8:22-31). It was also thought of in terms of cause, reason, mind – the very mind of God, the life-giving source, the eternal existence, the creative power which enabled the Word to become flesh.

In the Greek tradition, a tradition which was steeped in a rich intellectual heritage, there also existed a deeply profound concept of the Word which was called Logos. As well as meaning 'word', Logos also means 'reason'. For the Greek, the Logos was the mind of God who sustains the order of the whole universe; the Logos was the thought of God engraved upon the world. For the Greek, man's mind was stamped with the Logos; it was the Logos which gave the human being the power to think, to reason, to have knowledge. The Logos was not only the way by which God had made the world, but it was also the very mind of God who dwells within man, making him a thinking conscious being.

From this we can now begin to see something of the wonderful dynamic energy which flows from the Word of God – the creative force at work, the mastermind pervading and penetrating every aspect of our humanity, every particle of creation.

The New Testament teaches us how the Word became flesh (John 1:1-14). All that God spoke of in the Hebrew Scriptures reached fulfilment in his eternal Son, Jesus, who is the eternal Word become flesh within history. He wants to speak to us in a way that will change our lives. His Word calls us from darkness to light; from isolation to relationship; from division to unity; from separation to union.

He puts us in touch with our deepest needs in order to awaken us to realisation that 'Man does not live on bread alone but on every word that comes from the mouth of God' (Deuteronomy 8:3; Matthew 4:4).

As the Word begins to transform our lives, as the Holy Spirit internalises the Word in our hearts, we begin to experience wisdom and strength to release that Word into our ordinary everyday practical living and so to share it with others. '. . . and in a teachable spirit you must receive implanted in your heart the Word which is able to save your souls. You must not only listen to the Word; you must act on it. Otherwise, you indulge in self-deception . . .' (see James 1:21-25, adapted).

The two tables

The main parts of the Mass are called the Liturgy of the Word and the Liturgy of the Eucharist. In the Liturgy of the Word we hear the story of the people of God throughout the ages. We identify with their response to God's call – generous, indifferent or denied as in our own day. Of one and the same people, we are at one with those who have gone before us on the pilgrimage of faith. Now Christ, the Word of the Father, the Word made flesh, speaks to us of the Kingdom of God in our midst and of the Gospel values he calls us to live by. Words of life in an age that seeks for meaning (Matthew 13:13-17).

In the Liturgy of the Eucharist the same Jesus comes to us as the Bread of Life, food for our journey (John 6:51). He is the Bread that feeds and nourishes, enabling us to 'go in peace to love and serve the Lord', empowering us to make a lived response to his Word, working with him for the building of the Kingdom in today's society.

These complementary parts of the Mass are so closely related that they form one single act of worship. The idea is that we should move from one table to the other. At both we are nourished; at the one we are instructed by Christ the Teacher who plants the Word in our hearts, enabling it to become alive and active in our lives. 'It is written in the prophets: "They will all be taught by God," and to hear the teaching of the Father, and learn from it, is to come to me' (John 6:45). And at the other table we are fed by the same Christ, the Bread of Life. 'I am the living bread . . . anyone who eats this bread will live for ever' (John 6:51).

> The Church has always venerated the divine Scriptures just as she venerated the Body of the Lord; in so far as she never ceases, particularly in the Sacred Liturgy, to partake of the Bread of Life and to offer it to the faithful from the one table of the Word of God and the Body of Christ. *Paragraph 21, Dei Verbum,* Dogmatic Constitution on Divine Revelation.

> In the readings . . . God speaks to his people, reveals to them the mysteries of redemption and salvation, and provides them with spiritual nourishment; and Christ himself, in the form of his Word, is present in the midst of the faithful. *Paragraph 33, Cenam Paschalem,* General Instruction on the Roman Missal.

Consider also this quotation from one of the Early Church Fathers, Caesarius of Arles.

> I have a question for you, brothers and sisters. Which do you think more important – the Word of God or the Body of Christ? If you want to answer correctly, you must tell me that the Word of God is no less important than the Body of Christ! How careful

we are, when the Body of Christ is distributed to us, not to let any bit of it fall to the ground from our hand! But we should be just as careful not to let slip from our hearts the Word of God that is addressed to us, by thinking or speaking of something else. He will be no less guilty who listens negligently to the Word of God than he who by his negligence allows the Lord's Body to fall on the ground. *Caesarius of Arles, Sermon 78:2*

As we ponder on these things we come to realise that the ministry of reader is not just about getting up on Sunday or during the week and reading out the Scripture passages which we have only briefly looked at, but it becomes a God-given ministry, a response to God's call which brings about our own daily conversion – we come to realise that we are God's instrument, God is speaking his Word through us which is the Bread of life for all eternity.

... The Word of the Lord remains for ever. What is this Word? It is the Good News that has been brought to you (1 Peter 1:25).

Chapter 2 _____

_____ *Spiritual Preparation*

The ministry of reader

By virtue of our baptism we have the duty and privilege of spreading the Good News of salvation. Christ's command to 'Go out to the whole world: proclaim the Good News to all creation' (Mark 16:16) is addressed to every Christian. But among Christians there are some who have a special God-given gift for proclaiming his Word.

This ministry is specifically a lay ministry and the Church recognises:

• the need for the proclamation of God's Word

• that some people have a natural God-given ability to fulfil this need

• that those people need prayer, support and guidance to carry out this ministry

Aware of the office he has undertaken, the reader is to make every effort and employ suitable means to acquire that increasingly warm and living love and knowledge of Scripture that will make him a more perfect disciple of the Lord. *Motu proprio Ministeria quaedam of Pope Paul VI* on first tonsure, minor orders and the subdiaconate, 15 August 1972.

Before considering the more technical and practical aspects of this ministry let us look for a moment at those other things which are necessary and helpful to a reader, such as attitudes, basic commitments and the preparation and ways of praying the Scriptures.

Attitudes and commitments

The following is a list of some of the things which can lay the foundation stones in our ministry.

- Trust in God and in the power of the Holy Spirit to guide us
- A sense of reverence, dignity and privilege in the service of this sacred ministry
- Sincerity and humility
- The confidence to be ourselves with all our strengths and weaknesses
- Affirming ourselves and others in the gifts we have been given
- Realising that we are God's instruments and that he works through us and that we are actually part of the dialogue between God and his people

As the introduction to the Lectionary stresses, the reader is the instrument by which 'the Word constantly proclaimed in the liturgy is always a living, active Word through the power of the Holy Spirit. It expresses the Father's love that never fails in its effectiveness towards us.'

Understanding the proclamation of God's Word in this light can help to take us off the 'performer's platform' and bring us into the humbling spirit of this wonderful ministry.

Preparation of and praying the Scriptures

We have seen in the introduction that the ministry is about giving God's living Word back to the people – God's Word which is the source of all life: 'He is present in his Word since it is he himself who speaks when the holy Scriptures are read in the Church' (Paragraph 7, *Sacrosanctum Concilium,* The Constitution on the Sacred Liturgy). So the reader's true task is to enable the Word to become live and active in those who listen.

When we come to pray over Scripture we are not trying to develop our intellectual faculties. We are engaging in the perceptive, intuitive understanding of the heart – we listen with the ear of the heart. In this way we are able to journey more deeply into the mystery of the sacred source of this divine love.

Entering into this way of prayer we need an attitude of faith, an openness of heart and a deep desire to allow the action of the Holy Spirit to lead us ever more fully into this relationship of love. We need to dispose ourselves to allow the Word to take root in our hearts; the Word which teaches and nurtures us, helping us grow, enlightening and vitalising us.

Taking time out for prayer and for praying the Scriptures is not easy in today's world with all its distractions. It is, however, of vital importance. Somehow we have to make time to get off the fast track, with all its over-stimulation, passing attractions and business, which can create such restlessness, discontent and stress in us. We need to slow down in order to enter that secret place where such love, such joy and tenderness await to embrace us.

For our prayer we need time to come to stillness, to listen, to dispose ourselves and to let go of those things which hinder the growth of God's love within us. As in any growing relationship, we need to give 'the other' our time; to be 'in him in whom we live and move and have our being' (Acts 17:28).

Jesus tells us to 'go to your private room and, when you have shut your door, pray to your Father who is in that secret place, and your Father who sees all that is done in secret will reward you' (Matthew 6:6).

These words of Jesus tell us so much about prayer. They are words which invite us to enter into the interior quiet room of our hearts, that secret place where we can open ourselves to the Spirit of love deep within our being.

It is only when we have experienced this life-giving Spirit

through prayer and the Word of God in Scripture that we will thirst for more. We will come to embrace our prayer time with love and thanksgiving as we begin to realise what wonderful gifts are lavished upon us and what strength is given to help us to 'go and make the people of all nations my disciples' (Matthew 28:19).

So how do we approach praying the Scriptures? Many people will have found, and are happy with, their own particular way of praying over Scripture, but for those who are seeking new paths the following two ways may be helpful. They both come from very ancient traditions and have greatly enlightened and enriched men and women over the centuries in their understanding of Scripture. It must be stressed, though, that there are many different ways of praying and we will no doubt try many paths before finding the particular one which is right for us. In the end we will pray as we can, not as we can't.

Imaginative contemplation of Scripture

We tend to think of biblical stories as being only in the past; an event in history which has very little to do with us now in our present day. However, in order to make these stories catch fire and become alive and vibrant, it can be helpful to experience them in the light of our own life stories. This is where imaginative contemplation of Scripture will open up the creativity within us which may be partly dormant or have become dulled in adulthood. We need to awaken and nurture the imaginative, creative and feeling side of our nature. In contemplating biblical stories there can be a fusing of the past historical stories into our own present-day stories – stories which are a melting pot of hopes, hurts, woundedness, joys, sorrows, dreams.

Contemplating Scripture in an imaginative way has a long tradition. It is very much rooted in Ignatian spirituality which has come down to us from the sixteenth century. It goes back, however, even further than this. Ludolph of Saxony was a Carthusian monk who lived in the fourteenth century and he describes this way of prayer in the preface to his *Vita Christi*:

> Be present at Jesus' birth like another witness and rejoice with the Virgin Mother new with child for you. . . . Help his parents carry the child and present him in the temple. Alongside the apostles, accompany the Good Shepherd as he performs his miracles. Be there at his death. . . . Touch his body, handling one by one the wounds of your Saviour who died for you. With Mary Magdalene, seek the risen Christ. . . . If you want to draw fruit from these mysteries, you must offer yourself as present to what was said and done through our Lord Jesus Christ with the whole affective power of your mind. . . . Hear and see these things being narrated, as though you were hearing with your own ears and seeing with your own eyes. . . . Although these things are narrated as past events, you must meditate them all as though they were happening now. . . . Then you will feel how full of wisdom and delight they are.

What beautiful guidelines this Carthusian monk has handed down to us! We understand from this preface that it is possible to enter into the Scripture scene by way of our imagination and even by way of our senses.

The Gospel scenes are especially suitable for this kind of contemplation and it is important to remember that, in the Liturgy of the Word, the first reading is deliberately and carefully chosen to illustrate some aspect of the Gospel. This is why we need to meditate not only on the texts we shall be reading but also on the Gospel passage itself, which will give us a deeper understanding of the other readings. One last point regarding the first reading, the Psalm and the second reading: it is helpful to read not only the texts themselves but to read around the passages – the chapters from which they are taken – what comes before and after. This will give added insight into the texts which necessarily have to be taken out of context for the readings at Mass.

And so we come to our time of prayer. You may find it helpful to prepare in the following way:

- Find a place where you can be quiet and undisturbed in order to open yourself to the presence of God, declaring your dependency on him.
- Ask for the gift of understanding and enlightenment, for the gift of trust and confidence in God's love, and for a readiness to let God speak to you and to teach you to pray.
- Take the texts and read them slowly several times.

For imaginative contemplation look at the scene with your mind's eye and ask yourself:

- Is the scene in a town or in the country?
- What is the landscape like?
- What are the people doing?
- What are they talking about?

When the scene becomes alive for us in this way, we can then engage in imaginary conversation with the characters. We will enter fully into the scene. We will encounter Jesus, who enlightened and healed two thousand years ago, and who continues to heal and enlighten us in the here and now, who directly relates to the events and circumstances of our everyday life. We have moved from being just an observer on the sidelines to being fully involved in the story, which, although begun in the past, is ever-unfolding and breaking through into the present.

We may find that distractions come into the scene – our own life experiences mingling with that of the biblical scene. These may enable us to be drawn more fully and enter more deeply into the experience. They become part of the contemplation. We let the imagination lead, but we keep returning to the focus of our attention, which will always be leading us to a deeper relationship with Jesus, with God.

There will be some texts which are not necessarily pictorial or visual but are more abstract in substance, as in some of the Letters of St Paul. The imagination can still be at work here, but it will perhaps be more at a feeling, intuitive, perceptive level. The words from the Scripture passage will be drawn down from the mind, with its intellectual, rational, logical concepts and understanding, into the heart, which will break into and touch the deeper levels of consciousness.

We can see then that if we actively use our imagination with an attitude of faith, trust and a desire to come closer in our relationship to God, we enable ourselves to be more open to the power and mystery of God within our being and to his transforming love within us. 'Glory be to him whose power, working in us, can do infinitely more than we can ask or imagine' (Ephesians 3:20).

Lectio Divina: reading-meditating-praying

This second way of praying the Scriptures has a long history and is associated particularly with the Benedictines. In the days when books were few and not many people could read, a monk would stand up and read to his community a passage of Scripture slowly, repeating it over and over again. One by one, the monks would get up and go out, not because they were bored, or because they thought badly of the reading, but because they had got hold of a word, a phrase they could savour. Their prayer had begun.

Saint Benedict (AD 480-547) tells us that our time with Scripture is a 'spiritual reading vacation; a time set aside to waste time with God; a time to holiday with Christ.' Saint Benedict inherited this method of prayer, Lectio Divina, from the Desert Fathers via Cassian. At the end of the fourth and beginning of the fifth century, Cassian was a link between the Desert Fathers and western monasticism. His aim was unceasing prayer. In his *Institutes and Conferences*, he expounds praying the Scriptures. He describes it as the way to be ever mindful of God and to progress toward purity of heart.

> It is the poverty of the verse that is the key. There is the depen-
> dence on Christ and helplessness expressed by the words
> themselves, certainly, but more significant is the poverty of
> clinging to those few words from the Word of God rather
> than to the 'rich and full material of all manner of thoughts'.
> Choosing attentiveness rather than inquisitiveness, one fulfils
> the beatitude, 'Blessed are the poor in spirit'; one acquires
> innocence and discernment and is prepared for true knowledge
> of God.

We see then that this is a very different way of praying over Scripture from the pictorial, visual one where we engage the imagination in as much richness as possible. This is perhaps a more difficult way of prayer for us in the west, as we tend to have such busy, distracted, complex minds. It is a way of prayer, though, which can do much to lead us to stillness, to simplicity. 'Be still and know that I am God' (Psalm 46:10).

The Lectio Divina is a beautiful way of praying the Scriptures because, in each reading, we are given a gift which is uniquely personal to us, the gift being a word, or phrase, or an idea, which God is communicating to us and planting in our hearts. Savouring and pondering on this, we find that it can resonate and integrate with our ordinary everyday life. Also, the stilling of the mind is important, as it takes the spotlight off ourselves, off the ever-seeking ego and allows us to be centred in 'the other'. 'If anyone wishes to be a follower of mine he must leave self behind' (Matthew 16:24), Jesus said, and, 'In your prayer do not go babbling on like the heathen, who imagine that the more they say the more likely they are to be heard' (Matthew 6:7).

Although this way of praying can be used with almost any text in Scripture, it would seem very suited to those parts of the Old and New Testament which are reflective and contemplative, and would be appropriate for certain Psalms, Wisdom literature, passages from Isaiah, from St John, and some of the texts from the letters of St Paul.

So, for the Lectio Divina prayer time, you can prepare in the same way as you prepared for the imaginative contemplation, by going through the three preliminary stages of preparation described earlier.

When you have read through the text several times you may find that you notice in particular a certain word or phrase which will, as it were, 'leap out of the page'. This will be God's Word, alive and active, communicating with you – God personally addressing you in the here and now. As you read the text, dwell upon and savour those words and phrases which have been shown to you, to which you have felt drawn.

You may find that distractions come into your mind from the daily events of your life and will mingle with the reading. Acknowledge the distractions but move gently back to the reading, to the word or phrase to which you have felt drawn, and slowly keep repeating it over and over again, letting it flood your whole being. It has been likened to 'chewing the cud'.

Contemplating the Word of God in this way is just one of the many ways in which our love of Scripture will be developed. It will give us new insight and a deeper understanding of ourselves, of others and of our relationship with God, who is within our being and is part of every aspect of our lives. The Word will become for us a heartfelt experience and this will be reflected in the way we read. We will come to 'own' the Scripture passages and, as we do so, the passages will become more meaningful and communicate more strongly with those who listen.

> In the beginning was the Word:
> the Word was with God
> and the Word was God . . .
>
> The Word was made flesh,
> he lived among us,
> and we saw his glory,
> the glory that is his as the only son of the Father,
> full of grace and truth.
> (John 1:1, 14)

Chapter 3 _____

_____ *Practical Preparation*

Voice mechanism and breath control

It is God who calls us to ministry and so he calls certain people to be readers – to proclaim his Word in the celebration of the Mass.

The human voice is one of the most remarkable and beautiful instruments that we have. It is important, however, to understand something of its mechanism and its potential. We may possess a lightweight, soft-grained type of voice or a very incisive strong voice – either way we need to know how to manage it in relation to the style of the text, to the size of the church, the number of people in the congregation and to the particular microphone which we will be using. Without going into too much detail, let us consider briefly some of the things to aim at which will help us in proclaiming God's Word to the assembly.

Do remember at this point that we always need to be ourselves, acknowledging and affirming everything that makes us the unique person that we are. We need to keep this in mind as, delving more deeply, we strive to develop our ministry.

Reading out aloud is no use if the sound of the voice is not heard. The key to volume or loudness in speaking is breath control. We only need to know one or two things about our breathing and the most important thing to know is that when we breathe in, the air expands the ribcage like a balloon and the diaphragm goes down and out, *not* in and up. We also need to be aware that the abdominal muscles act as the 'legs' or the support of our voice production; we allow these muscles to pull down and outwards thus allowing the diaphragm more room to expand to the very base. So we need a deep low intake of breath and the ability to release that intake in a gradual and controlled way.

This control of the muscles on the outgoing breath, which gradually permits the diaphragm and ribcage to return to their original positions, allows the voice to be firmly rooted and to be well supported by a controlled steady pressure of breath. However, don't worry too much about 'feeling' all this – just keep breathing, knowing that we expand like a pair of bellows in the rib and stomach area on the intake of breath, and all will be well!

Another essential part of good breathing is our posture, which is of the utmost importance. Without feeling rigid, we need to feel that our bodies are in a stretched, alert and fully upright position. In this way, we affirm our personhood, the gift of life. 'You are the light of the world' (Matthew 5:14). 'You will shine in the world like bright stars because you are offering it the Word of Life' (Philippians 2:15-16).

Practising aloud

Until we have become experienced in public reading, practising aloud by ourselves or together with a friend who can offer positive criticism, will help us to understand in just how many different and varied ways we can use our voice. It will enable us to practice the breath control for some of the very long Pauline sentences and phrases which we come across in the second reading. It is also helpful, while practising, to paraphrase those difficult phrases and make the punctuation our own, in order to understand more clearly Paul's message.

Reading aloud will also help us to realise just how much we need to articulate the consonants and the ends of words – how important it is to understand that it is the tongue which gives clear diction and not just an over-mouthing of the words. These vowels and consonants are the very building blocks of our speech and they need to be well articulated so that our readings become vibrant and clear.

Working with a tape recorder can also have its uses and can help us in things such as tempo, articulation, colour and so on. It must be said, however, that this way of practice is not for everyone. Another area which can be helped by practising aloud is the pronunciation of difficult names, which can lead to much stumbling if we have not already got our tongues around them in the privacy of our home. They need to be practised really slowly, the tongue becoming familiar with each syllable. You will find a guide for the pronunciation of biblical names in Appendix 3 at the back of this handbook.

Voice modulation

Practice also helps us to improve on voice modulation. There are three basic ways to do this:

- changing the speed of speaking
- changing the pitch of the voice
- changing the volume and intensity of the voice

In public speaking it is absolutely essential to speak more slowly than in normal conversation; the actual delivery must be slower, giving time to sound each syllable clearly. However, bearing in mind the slower speed, one still needs to modulate the reading by varying the pace. For example, faster reading can indicate excitement; reading more slowly can give emphasis to different words and statements.

We also need to be confident about regulating our voice to suit the meaning and mood of the texts which we have already experienced in a heartfelt way as we prayed over and prepared our readings at home. We are delivering not just words, but a message. A flat, dull, monotonous delivery reduces Scripture to mere words, and will soon put people off listening. We will have killed the message. We have to learn to read with expression, modulating and inflecting our voice, using subtle little changes in the volume and speed of our delivery, so that the words have life. We must allow God to communicate his Word through us with all the colour, love, passion and beauty of which we are capable.

Pauses and silences

There are three particularly useful ways to employ pauses.

Initial pause

It is very important to pause before you begin. Inexperienced readers launch into their readings immediately, with the result that the first two or three lines are lost. Try not to begin until you feel that people have settled down and are ready to listen attentively. Look up and then announce 'a reading from . . .', pause for a moment, and then begin the reading. When you have finished the reading, pause for a moment, look up and then say, 'This is the Word of the Lord'.

Looking up and getting our heads out of the Lectionary is most important and we should always strive to do this at least at the beginning and at the end of our readings. Remember that we are the instrument of the personal dialogue between God and his people, so we need to address the people as personally as we can.

Dividing pauses

The length of pauses here should vary to express the degree of division or diversity of thought. They are also used to divide paragraphs and phrases and are used for punctuation marks.

Stress pauses

We can use pauses to highlight different words or short phrases. This will bring out a dramatic point which will give weight to what we are reading.

Don't be afraid of silence. God also dwells there. As Meister Eckhart, that great medieval mystic, writes, 'Nothing in all creation is so like God as stillness'. It is very helpful for the listener if there is a short silence before and after the psalm, and before the Gospel Acclamation, to allow people to reflect briefly on what they have heard. This gives time for the words to sink in and take root, giving nourishment to sustain people as they go about their daily lives. As readers we are not just reading the Word, but feeding the Word to those who listen.

Regional and ethnic accents

It is important to value, respect and affirm regional and ethnic accents. They are part of our roots and the rich heritage which we all share. We should be proud that they are still preserved in our mother sound. Fortunately, Britain is still very rich in accents and dialects. It must be said, however, that these native sounds have been and still can be undermined, neutralised by 'class', by schools and by the media. These problems go very deep into our social structures and touch on many complex and sensitive issues. Suffice it to say that we need always to value and celebrate the richness and variety of our mother sounds and not be discouraged if we should ever encounter prejudice. Having said this, however, it is possible that an accent or dialect is so pronounced and broad that it makes it very difficult for the congregation to understand what the reading is about. In this case professional advice and help should be sought.

Fear and nerves

Fear and nerves can play a great part in inhibiting the free flow of the voice which, instead of being able to function in a flexible and natural way, can become tight, monotone and restricted.

This can be helped by our attitudes, for example, that we are among friends and that God is using our gifts for his purpose. Calm, slow breathing before we get up to read can also help to quieten us down so that we are more physically in control, and it cannot be stressed enough that practising aloud at home will help enormously with our confidence.

Eye contact

It is said that the eye is the mirror of the soul. If this is so, then we do need to get our heads up and out of the Lectionary as much as possible. It is important to stress that 'eye contact' in the context of this ministry is about general visual contact with the congregation and not about a 'one-to-one' eye contact. It can help us if we have an imaginary person just beyond the last row of the church and, as our eyes are directed over the congregation towards this point, it gives the impression that everyone is being addressed.

As we become familiar with our texts there will be many phrases and words which we will want to share with people by looking up. This does strengthen communication and make something that has been shown to us in a heartfelt way in our prayer time come even further to life. This of course needs experience, courage and confidence, but it is something which we can work towards. We can start in a small way, as has already been suggested, by looking up at the beginning and ending of our readings. When we have got used to that, we could then decide on just one word or phrase which we would want to share more fully by looking up. It is helpful to use a finger to mark the place in the Lectionary when we look away from the book. In this way we ensure we do not lose our place when we look down again. Some lecterns need a small block of wood to site the Lectionary a little higher up on the lectern, thus making it easier for the reader's head to be raised, allowing the people listening to see not just the top of our heads, but the whole of our face. This is very important as our whole countenance can express and radiate in a fully human way the very creativeness of the Word of God in Scripture.

The use of the microphone

As has already been said we *must* be heard. It can seem strange hearing our own voice amplified, and this may inhibit us from proclaiming the Word in a strong and confident manner.

Let us for a moment think back to the time of Jesus. In his day there were no microphones and so people were used to using their voices in a very strong and projected way. What a wonderfully powerful voice Jesus himself must have had, as he spoke to the crowds – with what vitality, urgency and passion he must have spoken as he inspired his listeners with his proclamation of the Kingdom. Thinking back and contemplating these things can inspire us in our own ministry as we come into the understanding that we are indeed speaking on behalf of the writers of the Old and New Testaments.

Do check with the priest or sacristan that the microphone system is all switched on. Regarding the amplification of your voice, if you possess a lightweight voice you will have to move nearer to the microphone and if you have a strong incisive voice you will have to move away slightly. This can be practised beforehand with a trusted friend when the church is empty. But remember that, when the church is full, you will need more volume and will need to project just that little bit more than in an empty building.

A useful exercise is to practise the readings in the church without the microphone. You will be aware of how very much harder you have to work on everything and this includes the very soft speaking which is so important for emphasis. Speaking softly to underline important points can be just as effective as something said very loudly, but it still requires energy and the right kind of projection. When you return to the microphone again with the same reading, notice how much easier everything is – the whole thing will be more energised and confident.

Distractions

There is nothing very much we can do about distractions except to know that they will happen – babies crying; children falling off pews; people with loud hacking coughs and so on. In these circumstances the most important thing is to keep the concentration going as strongly as possible and focus even more on what the message of the text is saying, rather than being drawn into distractions.

Dress

If we have a sense of reverence and dignity towards the exercise of this sacred ministry then we will want to dress appropriately. If the attention of the listener is drawn visually towards a mode of dress which is flamboyant and over-revealing, or on the other hand, is very sloppy and untidy, then the listener will be distracted and will find it more difficult to concentrate and be drawn fully into the Scripture reading. So dress should always be discreet.

At a glance

Here is a list of words beginning with 'P' which can act as quick reminders of important facets of this ministry:

Prayer   Praise

Preparation   Proclamation

Practice	Posture
Pleasure	Passion
Pause	Pace
Pitch	Punctuation
Parentheses	Paragraphs
Phrasing	Power (of the Word)
Presence (of God)	

Reading about all this process of preparation can seem terribly daunting, but putting it into practice will, of course, take much less time and become easier the more experienced we become as readers. We must always remember anyway that, like prayer, we read as we can and not as we can't. 'As for the part in the rich soil, this is people with a noble and generous heart who have heard the Word and take it to themselves and yield a harvest through their perseverance' (Luke 8:15).

Chapter 4 _____

_____ *The Lectionary*

It is important to know the way round the three volumes of the Lectionary which are used at Mass.

Volume 1 (red binding) covers all Sundays and Solemnities plus the weekdays of the Advent, Christmas, Lent and Easter seasons.

Volume 2 (blue binding) covers the weekdays of Ordinary Time and saints' days.

Volume 3 (brown binding) has readings for special occasions.

The Sunday readings follow a three-year cycle, Years A, B and C. For Year A most of the Gospel readings are taken from St Matthew; Year B belongs to St Mark and Year C to St Luke. These three synoptic gospels (synoptic meaning 'with the same view' or literally 'able to be seen together'), deal with our Lord's public life and teaching. The Gospel of St John concentrates more on the deeper spiritual significance of Jesus' life and it is always St John's account of the Passion that we hear on Good Friday. Other extracts from St John's Gospel are read every year on the weekdays of Lent and Easter and from the seventeenth to the twenty-first Sundays of Year B.

For the weekday readings there is a two-year cycle. However, the Gospel readings are arranged in a single cycle and are repeated each year. Also the weekday readings for Advent and Lent are the same each year. Year I is used during odd-numbered years; Year II during even-numbered years.

The readings for the Mass are chosen with great care and on Sundays follow a definite pattern. The first reading is usually taken from the Old Testament. As has already been said, this first reading has been deliberately and carefully chosen to illustrate some aspect of the Gospel of the day. Between Easter and Pentecost the first readings are not taken from the Old Testament but from the New Testament. These readings tell us about the growth of the first Christian communities as recorded in the Acts of the Apostles. The Psalm of the day has been chosen as a response to the first reading. The second reading concentrates on Christian living and many of these readings are taken from the Letters of St Paul.

It is helpful to see at a glance the continuity of the readings from Sunday to Sunday throughout the year. Having an overview of the way narrative and discourse are continued and developed will give us more background and will give depth to our readings when we know what has gone before and what is to follow.

The description of the order of readings and the tables from the General Introduction to the Lectionary are to be found in Appendix 2 which also provides all the information that one would need regarding the Sunday and weekday readings throughout the year.

We need to pause here for a moment and consider very briefly the wonderful variety and contrasting styles of the different writers which we find in Scripture.

Gerard W. Hughes writes in his book, *The God of Surprises,* that:

> The Old Testament may be described as a faith autobiography of Israel. The Jews reflected on their history, a very messy and shameful history, with its brief moment of glory under King David, its long years of infidelity to God, of defeat, humiliation and captivity. They began to see their history in a new way, as a history of salvation in and through disaster and tribulation. Salvation history still continues in you and me. The Spirit who lived in Jesus and raised him from the dead, now lives in us and is at work in the events of our lives.

The Bible then is a work of great historical interest, charting the history of the Jewish people over centuries and exploring the origins and growth of the Christian church. It is also a considerable work of literature, containing wonderful stories, beautiful poetry and songs, great struggles, exciting narratives and memorable characters. All these different styles have to be taken into account when we proclaim the Word of God to the assembly. There needs to be a difference in delivery between the poetry of a text from Isaiah and, for example, one of the Letters from St Paul, which would contrast strongly with the prayerful beauty of some of the Psalms. This is where technique can help our reading; where voice modulation can do so much to colour the different styles with which we have to deal.

Chapter 5 _____

_____ *Putting It into Practice*

Some general points about the Mass

Before Mass starts the readers should let the priest or MC know that they are present. They should check that the Lectionary is open at the correct place and that the microphone is switched on and, if possible, adjusted to the correct height. (Some microphones cannot be adjusted.) If there are two readers of different heights then the angle of the microphone, if it is an adjustable one, should be adjusted to suit the needs of each reader. If a reader is not very tall it will help if they stand on a small platform or stool so that they are properly seen and can proclaim the Word freely and openly rather than being hidden by the Lectionary. In addition, before the beginning of Mass, the readers should find out whether the Psalm or Gospel Acclamation are being sung.

Customs vary from parish to parish. The Church recommends that the reader should carry the Book of the Gospels or the Lectionary in the entrance procession (if no deacon is present). This is a vivid sign of Christ present in his Word coming into the midst of his people. If there is more than one reader, then both readers may enter in the procession with one of them carrying the Book. If it is the Book of the Gospels that is being carried then this is placed on the altar as a reminder that we are being fed from the Table of God's Word. It is then carried to the lectern in the Gospel procession. If the book is the Lectionary, the reader should place it directly on the lectern or ambo. Both readers may then take their places in the sanctuary, or, if desired, may go to their places in the body of the church.

If the readers are not part of the entrance procession, they should take their places in the main body of the church near the front.

Only once the opening prayer has finished and the people have responded 'Amen' and sat down, should you leave your place. To move only when the Introductory Rite is finished also emphasises that it has been concluded and the Liturgy of the Word is about to begin. A good general rule is that people should not be moving when some other action is taking place, thus making as little disturbance as possible.

Ideally the reader should move easily from the body of the church to the centre of the sanctuary, bow to the altar and then go to the lectern. Some parishes may have to adapt because of the particular layout of the church. It is common practice that, where there are two readers, both go to the sanctuary together, bow to the altar and take their places, one at the lectern, the other at a seat to the side of the lectern. If the Psalm is being sung, both readers sit together until the singing is finished. The second reader will then come to the lectern.

The above points refer to a normal-sized church. Naturally things will have to be adapted if the sanctuary is very small or if a small chapel is being used.

Read always from the Lectionary and never from a missalette or Mass booklet and do not read the phrase in italic printed after the title of the reading.

Start with the phrase 'A reading from . . .' exactly as printed and not 'The first reading is a reading from . . .'. At the end of the reading pause for a moment, look up and then say, 'This is the Word of the Lord'.

If the psalm is being sung, return to your place or take a seat in the sanctuary. If there are two readers then it is better to remain in the sanctuary. Ideally the psalm should be sung, but if it is being recited then it can be done in various ways (see *The General Instruction on the Lectionary* for full details).

a. The traditional method of reciting a psalm

There is no need to say 'the Responsorial Psalm' or 'the response is' because people know what it is. Read the response through once; the people will repeat the response after you. Then read through each verse of the psalm, with the people making the response after each verse. There are times, however, when the reader will need to repeat the response, while making it clear that it is the response, in order to help the congregation who may not be able to remember what the response is, especially if it is a long or an unusual one.

An alternative is to read the verses straight through with the response repeated only at the beginning and the end.

b. The common recitation method

Here the response can be said once by reader and people and then the people join in reciting out loud the verses of the psalm with the response once more at the end. A variation on this is for the two sides of the church to say alternative verses.

Check with the priest, before Mass begins, which method of reciting the psalm is being used. It cannot be overstressed that the best method is for the psalm to be sung and not said or replaced by a hymn.

Allow a brief pause before continuing with the next reading, if there is one. As in the first reading, start with the phrase 'A reading from . . .' and not 'the second reading is a reading from . . .'.

With regard to the Gospel Acclamation, the Lectionary stresses that this must be sung.

On Easter Sunday and Pentecost there is a Sequence (a form of hymn) which is obligatory. This comes after the second reading and before the Gospel Acclamation. Check with the priest whether it is to be read or sung. If it is to be sung as a hymn then it may need announcing. On Easter Sunday a hymn version is *Christ the Lord is risen today* or *Bring, all ye dear bought nations, bring,* while on Pentecost a hymn version is *Holy Spirit, Lord of light*. Settings of these hymns will be found in most hymn books. There are two other days on which there is a Sequence but on these occasions it is optional: the Solemnity of the Body and Blood of Christ (Thursday after Trinity Sunday) and the memorial of Our Lady of Sorrows (15 September).

For the Gospel, the Homily and the Profession of Faith, either return to your place in the body of the church or to a seat in the sanctuary. If you leave the sanctuary, it is always best to leave from the front, bowing to the altar before you depart. Walk slowly – there is no need to hurry. If there are two readers, both can remain in the sanctuary.

After the Profession of Faith (the creed), comes the General Intercession or Bidding Prayer. The priest briefly introduces the intercessions in the form of an invitation addressed to the congregation to pray. There follows a series of petitions or intentions which are read at the lectern by the deacon (if one is present) or by the reader who, if they returned to their seat in the main body of the church after the Gospel Acclamation, will now return to the lectern after the Creed.

The petitions are normally:

* for the needs of the Universal Church;
* for the needs of the nation and of the human race at large;
* for classes of people who have special needs;
* for the congregation and the local community.

At the end of each intention there should be a pause of about five seconds to allow people to pray before the reader seeks their response in one of the following ways:

Reader: Lord, hear us.
People: Lord, graciously hear us.
Or

Reader: Lord, in your mercy
People: hear our prayer.

Or

Reader:	We pray to the Lord.
People:	Lord, hear us
or	Lord, hear our prayer

or some similar response, perhaps based on a phrase from the readings of the day.

The reader may then invite the people to seek the help of Mary and lead the recitation of the 'Hail Mary'. After this the people are invited by the reader to pray for a short while in silence for their own needs and intentions. This silence may precede the Marian prayer and it may be concluded in the same way as the other intentions with 'Lord hear us . . .'. The reader should not use this silence to depart from the lectern back to their seat but should remain at the lectern until after the concluding prayer which is said by the priest. Only after this should the reader return to their place in the main body of the church, leaving the sanctuary, as before, from the centre front, and bowing to the altar as they depart.

The Entrance Antiphon and the Communion Antiphon

It is usual for a hymn to be sung at the beginning of the Mass but, if there is no music, it is helpful for the readers to lead the assembly in the recitation of the opening antiphon. Likewise with the communion antiphon, just as the priest is raising the chalice to his lips, the reader should lead the assembly in the recitation of the antiphon. After this the bell is rung to summon the people to receive communion.

If you cannot read on a day on which you are scheduled to read, try to arrange a substitute. If that is not possible then let the priest know well in advance that you will not be reading.

Chapter 6 _____

_____ *Conclusion*

As we come to the conclusion of these guidelines, let us think for a moment as to how a parish, in response to the needs of this ministry, could organise certain events which would nourish, support and encourage its readers.

Many parishes already have excellent programmes of events which have been on-going for years, but for those parishes who are seeking to set up some sort of renewal programme for the readers, days of Recollection and Readers' days on the importance of the ministry would be very helpful. These days would include, of course, all the practical and technical side of the ministry. There are many days arranged for ministers of the Eucharist to come together for renewal and prayer. If days could be organised for both ministries to come together to share in the Two Tables it would be a very enriching experience. The two ministries have so much to give each other and are so closely related that they form one single act of worship.

There could also be an annual event in which several parishes could collaborate together for discussion and group work, giving readers from the different parishes the opportunity to talk and share amongst themselves. This would also create a feeling of greater 'outreach' in the community. Workshops specially designed for young readers and for those with little experience could also be arranged.

It is important to encourage a proper commissioning of those who are to be readers in the community, and the *Rite of Commissioning Parish Readers* is just for this purpose. This Rite is for new readers but there is also a *Rite for the Renewal of Commitment* for people who are already ministers of the Word. You will find a formula for each of these Rites in Appendix 1 of this handbook. For further information see the *Southwark Liturgy Bulletin,* No 86, February 1994, and the book *Services for Church and Home.*

Some readers have organised Scripture groups in their own homes where they can study and share Scripture together. This has tremendous value; it is through one another that we learn and it is a great help to have the encouragement and support of others as we try to deepen our understanding of Scripture. As Jesus says, 'For where two or three are gathered in my name, there I am in the midst of them' (Matthew 18:20).

Let us end with a quote from John Wijngaards, writing about *Dei Verbum,* the Vatican II document on revelation:

> When God speaks to humankind, he employs human words. God speaking to us actually makes use of the words of Scripture. This is true whether we consider people at the time of Christ or in the Church today. God makes use of the words as they have been handed down (literally, 'tradition') by the Church, that is, in the actual Scriptures we possess. But the over-riding, eminently important and absolutely vital element in revelation is that we see it as the self-revelation of God himself. The words are only the occasion, the external symbol or sacrament, the lasting visible memorial of an event that is ever new. What matters in any and every part of Scripture is the contact with the living God himself.
>
> The experience of God to which the biblical authors bear witness ought to spark off in ourselves the living experience of God in our situation here and now. That is what revelation is about. The real meaning of the Bible, therefore, is in not the correct communication of abstract truths but in bringing about this new, live experience of God in our own days.' John Wijngaards, *Reading God's Word to Others.*

So let us hope that, through a deepening awareness and understanding of this wonderful ministry, the Word of God may become more alive and active in ourselves as readers and in the hearts of those who listen.

Out of his infinite glory, may he give you the power through his Spirit for your hidden self to grow strong, so that Christ may live in your hearts through faith, and then, planted in love and built on love, you will with all the saints have strength to grasp the breadth and the length, the height and the depth; until, knowing the love of Christ, which is beyond all knowledge, you are filled with the utter fullness of God.

Glory be to him whose power, working in us, can do infinitely more than we can ask or imagine; glory be to him from generation to generation in the Church and in Christ Jesus for ever and ever. AMEN. (Ephesians 3:16-21)

Appendix I _____

_____ *Commissioning of Parish Readers*

Most appropriately, this should take place during a Mass attended by the people and at a time when the Readers will exercise their function. It may be celebrated outside Mass. It is most appropriate at the end of a day of preparation of Readers.

The Homily should explain the place of the Word of God in the liturgy and the importance of proclaiming it well. After the Homily, those to be commissioned as Parish Readers are presented to the people in these or similar words:

Dear Friends in Christ,
our brothers and sisters *N* and *N* are to be given the great privilege of proclaiming God's Word in the Assembly. Through them, God will speak to his people of the salvation and redemption won for them by the Lord Jesus, so that, nourished by this Word, the people will grow in the love and the knowledge of God.

The celebrant pauses and then addresses the candidates:

You have been called to proclaim the Word of God in the assembled community of God's people and in so doing you are sharing in the Church's mission to preach the Good News to all peoples. May God's Word be living and active in your lives, that you may worship the living God in spirit and in truth.

In proclaiming God's Word to others, accept it yourself in obedience to the Holy Spirit. Meditate on it constantly, so that each day you will have a deeper love for the Scriptures and in all you say and do, show forth to the world our Saviour, Jesus Christ.

After the address, the candidates stand before the celebrant who asks them these questions:

Are you willing to become a Reader and to proclaim God's Word to the people assembled in this Church?

Response: I am.

Are you willing to prepare each proclaiming of God's Word by study and prayer?

Response: I am.

The celebrant then hands a Bible to a representative of the readers (or to all the readers) and prays:

Let us pray to God our loving Father and ask him to bless our brothers and sisters chosen to proclaim His Word:

God our Father, you have given our brothers and sisters faith in you and in your living Word. We ask you to help them grow in faith as they meditate upon your Word, so that they may worthily proclaim the Word to the Assembly and by the manner of their lives.

Rite of Renewal of Commitment of Parish Readers

Those who read publicly in church are exercising a liturgical ministry on behalf of the community they serve. It is appropriate that on a given day each year parish readers renew that commitment in the presence of the community, at the Mass which they normally attend. One such opportunity might be the Second Sunday of Advent which is kept as Bible Sunday.

The renewal takes place after the Homily. The people should be invited to remain seated.

The priest first addresses the people:

Priest: Dear friends in Christ,
our brothers and sisters have the great privilege
of proclaiming God's word in the assembly.
Through them God speaks to us, his people,
of the salvation and redemption won for us by the
    Lord Jesus
so that, nourished by this word,
we will grow in the love and knowledge of God.

The readers stand. If space permits they might come and stand in front of the altar. The priest addresses the readers:

Priest: Dear readers,
you have been called to proclaim the word of God.
In doing so you are sharing in the Church's mission
to preach the Good News to all people.
May God's word be living and active in your lives,
that you may worship the living God in spirit and truth.
In proclaiming God's word to others,
accept it yourself in obedience to the Holy Spirit.

Will you continue to exercise the ministry of reader,
proclaiming God's word to the people in this church?

Readers: I will.

Priest: Will you prepare yourselves each time you proclaim
God's word by prayer and study?

Readers: I will.

All now stand.

Priest: Let us pray to God our loving Father and ask him to
bless our brothers and sisters who proclaim his word.

There is a pause for silence.
The priest extends his hands over the readers.

Priest: God our Father,
you have given our brothers and sisters faith in you
and your living word.
We ask you to help them grow in that faith
so that they may worthily proclaim it to this assembly.
We ask this through Christ our Lord.

All: Amen.

*The Mass continues with the Profession of Faith (if it is a Sunday
or Solemnity) and the Bidding Prayer.*

Appendix 2 _____

_____ *Description of the Order of Readings*

It seems useful to provide here a brief description of the Order of Readings, at least for the principal celebrations and the different seasons of the liturgical year, as set out in the *General Introduction to the Lectionary.*

1. Advent

Sundays

Each Gospel reading has a distinctive theme: the Lord's coming at the end of time (First Sunday of Advent), John the Baptist (Second and Third Sunday), and the events that prepared immediately for the Lord's birth (Fourth Sunday).

The Old Testament readings are prophecies about the Messiah and the Messianic age, especially from Isaiah.

The readings from an apostle serve as exhortations and as proclamations, in keeping with the different themes of Advent.

Weekdays

There are two series of readings: one to be used from the beginning of Advent until 16 December; the other from 17 to 24 December.

In the first part of Advent there are readings from Isaiah, distributed in accord with the sequence of the book itself and including salient texts that are also read on the Sundays. For the choice of the weekday Gospel the first reading has been taken into consideration.

On Thursday of the second week the readings of the Gospel about John the Baptist begin. The first reading is either a continuation of Isaiah or a text chosen in view of the Gospel.

In the last week before Christmas the events that immediately prepared for the Lord's birth are presented from Matthew (Chapter 1) and Luke (Chapter 1). The texts in the first reading, chosen in view of the Gospel reading, are from different Old Testament books and include important Messianic prophecies.

2. Christmas season

Solemnities, Feasts, and Sundays

For the vigil and the three Masses of Christmas both the prophetic readings and the others have been chosen from the Roman tradition.

The Gospel on the Sunday within the octave of Christmas, feast of the Holy Family, is about Jesus' childhood and the other readings are about the virtues of family life.

On the octave of Christmas, solemnity of Mary, Mother of God, the readings are about the Virgin Mother of God and the giving of the holy Name of Jesus.

On the second Sunday after Christmas, the readings are about the mystery of the incarnation.

On Epiphany, the Old Testament reading and the Gospel continue the Roman tradition; the text for the reading from the apostolic letters is about the calling of all peoples to salvation.

On the feast of the Baptism of the Lord, the texts are chosen about this mystery.

Weekdays

From 29 December on, there is a continuous reading of the whole of 1 John, which actually begins earlier, on 27 December, feast of St. John the Evangelist, and on 28 December, feast of the Holy Innocents. The Gospels relate manifestations of the Lord: events of Jesus' childhood from Luke (29-30 December); passages from John 1 (31 December-5 January); other manifestations from the four Gospels (7-18 January).

3. Lent

Sundays

The Gospel readings are arranged as follows:

The first and second Sundays retain the accounts of the Lord's temptations and transfiguration, with readings, however, from all three Synoptics.

On the next three Sundays, the Gospels about the Samaritan woman, the man born blind, and the raising of Lazarus have been restored in Year A. Because these Gospels are of major importance in regard to Christian initiation, they may also be read in Year B and Year C, especially in places where there are catechumens.

Other texts, however, are provided for Year B and Year C: for Year B, a text from John about Christ's coming glorification through his cross and resurrection and for Year C, a text from Luke about conversion.

On Passion Sunday (Palm Sunday) the texts for the procession are selections from the Synoptic Gospels concerning the Lord's triumphal entrance into Jerusalem. For the Mass the reading is the account of the Lord's passion.

The Old Testament readings are about the history of salvation, which is one of the themes proper to the catechesis of Lent. The series of texts for each Year presents the main elements of salvation history from its beginning until the promise of the New Covenant.

The readings from the letters of the apostles have been selected to fit the Gospel and the Old Testament readings and, to the extent possible, to provide a connection between them.

Weekdays

The readings from the Gospels and the Old Testament were selected because they are related to each other. They treat various themes of the Lenten catechesis that are suited to the spiritual significance of this season. Beginning with Monday of the fourth week of Lent, there is a semicontinuous reading of the Gospel of John, made up of texts that correspond more closely to the themes proper to Lent.

Because the readings about the Samaritan woman, the man born blind, and the raising of Lazarus are now assigned to Sundays, but only for Year A (in Year B and Year C they are optional), provision has been made for their use on weekdays. Thus at the beginning of the Third, Fourth, and Fifth Weeks of Lent optional Masses with these texts for the Gospel have been inserted and may be used in place of the readings of the day on any weekday of the respective week.

In the first half of Holy Week the readings are about the mystery of Christ's passion. For the chrism Mass the readings bring out both Christ's messianic mission and its continuation in the Church by means of the sacraments.

4. The Easter Triduum and the Easter season

The Easter Triduum

On Holy Thursday at the evening Mass the remembrance of the supper preceding Christ's departure casts its own special light because of the Lord's example in washing the feet of his disciples and Paul's account of the institution of the Christian Passover in the Eucharist.

On Good Friday the liturgical service has as its centre John's narrative of the passion of him who was portrayed in Isaiah as the Servant of Yahweh and who became the one High Priest by offering himself to the Father.

On the holy night of the Easter Vigil there are seven Old Testament readings, recalling the wonderful works of God in the history of salvation. There are two New Testament readings, the announcement of the resurrection according to one of the Synoptic

Gospels and a reading from St. Paul on Christian Baptism as the sacrament of Christ's resurrection.

The Gospel reading for the Mass on Easter Day is from John on the finding of the empty tomb. There is also, however, the option to use the Gospel texts from the Easter Vigil or, when there is an evening Mass on Easter Sunday, to use the account in Luke of the Lord's appearance to the disciples on the road to Emmaus. The first reading is from Acts, which throughout the Easter season replaces the Old Testament reading. The reading from St. Paul concerns the living out of the paschal mystery in the Church.

Sundays

The Gospel readings for the first three Sundays recount the appearance of the risen Christ. The readings about the Good Shepherd are assigned to the Fourth Sunday. On the Fifth, Sixth, and Seventh Sundays, there are excerpts from the Lord's discourse and prayer at the Last Supper.

The first reading is from Acts, in a three-year cycle of parallel and progressive selections: material is presented on the life of the primitive Church, its witness, and its growth.

For the reading from the apostles, 1 Peter is in Year A, 1 John in Year B, Revelation in Year C. These are the texts that seem to fit in especially well with the spirit of joyous faith and sure hope proper to this season.

Weekdays

As on the Sundays, the first reading is a semicontinuous reading from Acts. The Gospel readings during the Easter octave are accounts of the Lord's appearances. After that there is a semicontinuous reading of the Gospel of John, but with texts that have a paschal character in order to complete the reading from John during Lent. This paschal reading is made up in large part of the Lord's discourse and prayer at the last supper.

Solemnities of the Ascension and Pentecost

For the first reading the solemnity of the Ascension retains the account of the Ascension according to Acts. This text is complemented by the second reading from the apostolic reflections on Christ in exultation at the right hand of the Father. For the Gospel reading, each of the three Years has its own text in accord with the differences in the Synoptic Gospels.

In the evening Mass celebrated on the Vigil of Pentecost four Old Testament texts are provided; any one of them may be used, in order to bring out the many aspects of Pentecost. The reading from the apostles shows the actual working of the Holy Spirit in the Church. The Gospel reading recalls the promise of the Spirit made by Christ before his own glorification.

For the Mass on Pentecost itself, in accord with received usage, the account in Acts of the great occurrence on Pentecost is taken as the first reading. The texts from Paul bring out the effect of the action of the Holy Spirit in the life of the Church. The Gospel reading is a remembrance of Jesus bestowing his Spirit on the disciples on Easter evening; other optional texts describe the action of the Spirit on the disciples and on the Church.

5. Ordinary Time

Arrangement and choice of texts

Ordinary Time begins on the Monday after the Sunday following 6 January; it lasts until the Tuesday before Lent inclusive. It begins again on the Monday after Pentecost Sunday and finishes before evening prayer I of the First Sunday of Advent.

The Order of Readings provides readings for thirty-four Sundays and the weeks following them. In some years, however, there are only thirty-three weeks of Ordinary Time. Further, some Sundays either belong to another season (the Sunday on which the feast of the Baptism of the Lord falls and Pentecost) or else are impeded by a solemnity that coincides with Sunday (for example, Holy Trinity or Christ the King).

For the correct arrangement in the use of the readings for Ordinary Time, the following are to be respected:

1. The Sunday on which the feast of the Baptism of the Lord falls replaces the First Sunday in Ordinary Time. Therefore the readings of the First Week of Ordinary Time begin on the Monday after the Sunday following 6 January. When the feast of the Baptism of the Lord is celebrated on Monday because Epiphany has been celebrated on the Sunday, the readings of the First Week begin on Tuesday.

2. The Sunday following the feast of the Baptism of the Lord is the Second Sunday of Ordinary Time. The remaining Sundays are numbered consecutively up to the Sunday preceding the beginning of Lent. The readings for the week in which Ash Wednesday falls are suspended after the Tuesday readings.

3. For the resumption of the readings of Ordinary Time after Pentecost Sunday:

When there are thirty-four Sundays in Ordinary Time, the week to be used is the one that immediately follows the last week used before Lent.

So, for example, when there are six weeks before Lent, the seventh week begins on the Monday after Pentecost. The solemnity of the Holy Trinity replaces the Sunday of Ordinary Time.

When there are thirty-three Sundays in Ordinary Time, the first week that would have been used after Pentecost is omitted, in order to reserve for the end of the year the eschatological texts that are assigned to the last two weeks.

When there are, for example, five weeks before Lent, the Monday after Pentecost begins with the Seventh Week of Ordinary Time and the Sixth Week is dropped.

Sunday readings

1 Gospel readings

On the Second Sunday of Ordinary Time the Gospel continues to centre on the manifestation of the Lord, which Epiphany celebrates through the traditional passage about the wedding feast at Cana and two other passages from John.

Beginning with the Third Sunday, there is a semicontinuous reading of the Synoptic Gospels. This reading is arranged in such a way that as the Lord's life and preaching unfold the teaching proper to each of these Gospels is presented.

This distribution also provides a certain co-ordination between the meaning of each Gospel and the progress of the liturgical year. Thus after Epiphany the readings are on the beginning of the Lord's preaching and they fit in well with Christ's baptism and the first events in which he manifests himself. The liturgical year leads quite naturally to a termination in the eschatological theme proper to the last Sundays, since the chapters of the Synoptics that precede the account of the passion treat this eschatological theme rather extensively.

After the Sixteenth Sunday in Year B, five readings are incorporated from John 6 (the discourse on the bread of life). This is the proper place for these readings because the multiplication of the loaves from John takes the place of the same account in Mark. In the semicontinuous reading of Luke for Year C, the introduction of this Gospel has been prefixed to the first text (that is, on the Third Sunday). This passage expresses the author's intention very beautifully and there seemed to be no better place for it.

2 Old Testament readings

These readings have been chosen to correspond to the Gospel passages in order to avoid an excessive diversity between the readings of different Masses and above all to bring out the unity between the Old and New Testament. The relationship between the readings of the same Mass is shown by a precise choice of the headings prefixed to the individual readings.

To the degree possible, the readings have been chosen in such a way that they would be short and easy to grasp. But care has been taken to ensure that many Old Testament texts of major significance would be read on Sundays. Such readings are distributed not according to a logical order but on the basis of what the Gospel reading requires. Still, the treasury of the Word of God will be opened up in such a way that nearly all the principal pages of the Old Testament will become familiar to those taking part in the Mass on Sundays.

3 Reading from the apostles

There is a semicontinuous reading of the Letters of Paul and James. (The Letters of Peter and John are read during the Easter and Christmas seasons.)

Because it is quite long and deals with such diverse issues, the First Letter to the Corinthians has been spread over the three years of the cycle at the beginning of Ordinary Time. It also was thought best to divide Hebrews into two parts; the first part is read in Year B and the second in Year C.

Only readings that are short and readily grasped by the people have been chosen.

Table IV at the end of the General Introduction to Volume 1 of the Lectionary indicates the distribution of letters of the apostles over the three-year cycle of the Sundays of Ordinary Time.

Readings for Solemnities of the Lord during Ordinary Time

On the solemnities of Holy Trinity, Corpus Christi, and the Sacred

Heart, the texts chosen correspond to the principal themes of these celebrations.

The readings of the Thirty-Fourth and last Sunday of Ordinary Time celebrate Christ the King. He was prefigured by David and heralded as king amid the humiliations of his passion and cross; he reigns in the Church and will come again at the end of time.

Weekday readings

1. The *Gospels* are so arranged that Mark is read first (First to Ninth Week), then Matthew (Tenth to Twenty-first Week), then Luke (Twenty-second to Thirty-fourth Week). Mark 1-12 are read in their entirety, with the exception only of the two passages of Mark 6 that are read on weekdays in other seasons. From Matthew and Luke the readings comprise all the matters not contained in Mark. From all three Synoptics or from two of them, as the case may be, all those passages are read that either are distinctively presented in each Gospel or are needed for a proper understanding of its progression. Jesus' eschatological discourse as contained in its entirety in Luke is read at the end of the liturgical year.

2. The first reading is taken in periods of weeks from the Old then from the New Testament; the number of weeks depends on the length of the biblical books read.

   Rather large sections are read from the New Testament books in order to give the substance, as it were, of each of the letters of the apostles.

   From the Old Testament there is room only for select passages that, as far as possible, bring out the character of the individual books. The historical texts have been chosen in such a way as to provide an overall view of the history of salvation before the Lord's incarnation. But lengthy narratives could hardly be presented; sometimes verses have been selected that make for a reading of moderate length. In addition, the religious significance of the historical events is sometimes brought out by means of certain texts from the wisdom books that are placed as prologues or conclusions to a series of historical readings.

Nearly all the Old Testament books have found a place in the Order of Readings for weekdays in the Proper of Seasons. The only omissions are the shortest of the prophetic books (Obadiah and Zephaniah) and the poetic book (Song of Solomon). Of those narratives written to edify and requiring a rather long reading to be understood, Tobit and Ruth are included, but Esther and Judith are omitted. (Texts from these two books are assigned to Sundays and weekdays at other times of the year.)

Tables are given to list the way the books of the Old and the New Testament are distributed over the weekdays in Ordinary Time in the course of two years.

At the end of the liturgical year the readings are from Daniel and Apocalypse, the books that correspond to the eschatological character of this period.

Table I
Order for Gospel reading for Sundays in Ordinary Time
YEAR A: YEAR OF MATTHEW

In order to do justice to the intention of the Lectionary, the five great 'sermons' in Matthew's Gospel will of necessity be the focal points of preaching and instruction. The narrative sections, which are placed in between the sermons, are composed in such a way that there is a unity and coherence in the whole work. Discourse and narrative stand side by side, so that narrative chapters prepare the way for what follows in the discourses. Recognising the way in which the Lectionary has reflected the structure of Matthew's Gospel will enable preachers and readers to see the context of the readings from one week to the next.

	The Figure of Jesus the Messiah	**Sundays 1-2**
SUNDAY 1	The Baptism of Jesus	Matthew3:13-17
SUNDAY 2	The witness of John the Baptist	John 1:29-34

	Christ's design for life in God's Kingdom	**Sundays 3-9**
	Narrative:	
SUNDAY 3	The call of the first disciples	Matthew 4:12-23
	Discourse:	
SUNDAY 4	The Sermon on the Mount (1)	Matthew 5:1-12
SUNDAY 5	The Sermon on the Mount (2)	Matthew 5:13-16
SUNDAY 6	The Sermon on the Mount (3)	Matthew 5:17-37
SUNDAY 7	The Sermon on the Mount (4)	Matthew 5:38-48
SUNDAY 8	The Sermon on the Mount (5)	Matthew 6:24-34
SUNDAY 9	The Sermon on the Mount (6)	Matthew 7:21-27

	The spread of God's Kingdom	**Sundays 10-13**
	Narrative:	
SUNDAY 10	The call of Levi	Matthew 9:9-13

	Discourse:	
SUNDAY 11	The mission sermon (1)	Mathew 9:36-10:8
SUNDAY 12	The mission sermon (2)	Matthew 10:26-33
SUNDAY 13	The mission sermon (3)	Matthew 10:37-42

The mystery of God's Kingdom   **Sundays 14-17**

	Narrative:	
SUNDAY 14	The revelation to the simple	Matthew 11:25-30

	Discourse:	
SUNDAY 15	The parable sermon (1)	Matthew 13:1-23
SUNDAY 16	The parable sermon (2)	Matthew 13:24-43
SUNDAY 17	The parable sermon (3)	Matthew 13:44-52

God's Kingdom on earth –
The Church of Christ   **Sundays 18-24**

	Narrative:	
SUNDAY 18	Feeding of five thousand	Matthew 14:31-21
SUNDAY 19	Jesus walks on the waters	Matthew 14:22-33
SUNDAY 20	The Canaanite woman	Matthew 15:21-28
SUNDAY 21	Peter's confession:	
	the primacy conferred	Matthew 16:13-20
SUNDAY 22	The passion prophesied:	
	discipleship	Matthew 16:21-27

	Discourse:	
SUNDAY 23	The community sermon (1)	Matthew 18:15-20
SUNDAY 24	The community sermon (2)	Matthew 18:21-35

Authority and invitation –
the ministry ends   **Sundays 25-33**

	Narrative:	
SUNDAY 25	The parable of the labourers	Matthew 20:1-16
SUNDAY 26	The parable of the two sons	Matthew 21:28-32
SUNDAY 27	The parable of the wicked	
	vinedressers	Matthew 21:33-43
SUNDAY 28	The parable of the marriage feast	Matthew 22:1-14
SUNDAY 29	Paying tribute to Caesar	Matthew 22:15-21
SUNDAY 30	The greatest commandment	Matthew 22:34-40
SUNDAY 31	Hypocrisy and ambition	Matthew 23:1-12

	Discourse:	
SUNDAY 32	The final sermon (1)	Matthew 25:1-13
SUNDAY 33	The final sermon (2)	Matthew 25:14-30
	God's Kingdom fulfilled	**Sunday 34**
SUNDAY 34	Christ the King	Matthew 25:31-46

Table II
Order for Gospel reading for Sundays in Ordinary Time
YEAR B: YEAR OF MARK

Mark's main interest is the person of Jesus himself. He follows Jesus through his public ministry in Galilee, outside Galilee and finally in Jerusalem itself immediately before the passion. The crisis is reached when the fundamental question is posed to the disciples: 'Who do you say I am?' Peter's confession of faith is, therefore, at the heart of Mark's Gospel. In the year of Mark the Lectionary observes faithfully the structure and message of the Gospel itself. One important peculiarity is that the Lectionary includes a major insert from the Gospel of John (Sundays 17-21: John 6 – the sermon on the 'Bread of Life'). This fits well into this part of Mark's Gospel, which is concerned with Jesus' revelation of himself, and is known as 'the Bread section'.

	The figure of Jesus the Messiah	**Sundays 1-2**
SUNDAY 1	The baptism of Jesus	Mark 1:6b-11
SUNDAY 2	The call of Andrew	
	and his friend	John 1:35-42
	The Mystery progressively revealed	**Sundays 3-23**
Stage I	*Jesus with the Jewish crowds*	*Sundays 3-9*

SUNDAY 3	The call of the first apostles	Mark 1:14-20
SUNDAY 4	A day in Capernaum (1)	Mark 1:21-28
SUNDAY 5	A day in Capernaum (2)	Mark 1:29-39
SUNDAY 6	The cure of a leper	Mark 1:40-45
SUNDAY 7	The cure of a paralytic	Mark 2:1-12
SUNDAY 8	The question of fasting	Mark 2:18-22
SUNDAY 9	Violation of the Sabbath	Mark 2:23-3:6
Stage II	*Jesus with his disciples*	*Sundays 10-14*
SUNDAY 10	Serious criticism of Jesus	Mark 3:20-35
SUNDAY 11	The parables of the Kingdom	Mark 4:26-34
SUNDAY 12	The calming of the storm	Mark 4:35-41
SUNDAY 13	Jairus' daughter;	
	the woman in the crowd	Mark 5:21-43
SUNDAY 14	Jesus rejected at Nazareth	Mark 6:1-6
Stage III	*Jesus manifests himself*	*Sundays 15-23*
SUNDAY 15	The mission of the twelve	Mark 6:7-13
SUNDAY 16	Compassion for the crowds	Mark 6:30-34
SUNDAY 17	The feeding of five thousand	John 6:1-15
SUNDAY 18	The bread of life (1)	John 6:24-35
SUNDAY 19	The bread of life (2)	John 6:41-52
SUNDAY 20	The Eucharist	John 6:51-58
SUNDAY 21	Incredulity and faith	John 6:61-70
SUNDAY 22	Jewish customs	Mark 7:1-8, 14-15, 21
SUNDAY 23	The cure of a deaf-mute	Mark 7:31-37
	The Mystery of the Son of Man	**Sundays 24-34**
Stage I	*The 'Way' of the Son of Man*	*Sundays 24-30*
SUNDAY 24	Peter's confession of faith	Mark 8:27-35
SUNDAY 25	Passion and resurrection prophesied	Mark 9:29-36
SUNDAY 26	Instructions for disciples	Mark 9:37-42, 44, 46-47
SUNDAY 27	Marriage and divorce	Mark 10:2-16
SUNDAY 28	The problem of wealth	Mark 10:17-30
SUNDAY 29	The sons of Zebedee	Mark 10:35-46
SUNDAY 30	The cure of Bartimaeus	Mark 10:46-52
Stage II	*Final revelation in Jerusalem*	*Sundays 31-33*
SUNDAY 31	The first commandment	Mark 12:28b-34

SUNDAY 32	The widow's mite	Mark 12:38-44
SUNDAY 33	The last things	Mark 13:24-32
Stage III	*The fulfilment of the mystery*	*Sunday 34*
SUNDAY 34	The solemnity of Christ the king	John18:33b-37

Table III
Order for Gospel reading for Sundays in Ordinary Time
YEAR C: YEAR OF LUKE

Luke's Gospel represents Jesus' journey from Galilee to Jerusalem – a journey which is completed in the Acts of the Apostles by the journey of the Church from Jerusalem 'to the ends of the earth'. The Lectionary in the year of Luke represents faithfully his 'Travel Narrative' (chapters 9-19) – Jesus' journey to death, to resurrection and his return to the Father (see Sundays 13-31). Luke's vision of the journey is not geographical or chronological. Rather it is seen as a journey for the whole Church and for the individual Christian, a journey towards suffering and glory. Each Gospel passage should mean a great deal more to preacher and reader when it is seen in the context of the whole programme of readings for Year C.

* Passages marked with an asterisk are found only in the Gospel of Luke.

	The figure of Jesus the Messiah	**Sundays 1-2**
SUNDAY 1	The baptism of Jesus	Luke 3:15-16, 21-22
SUNDAY 2	The marriage feast at Cana	John 2:1-12
	Luke's programme for Jesus' ministry	**Sundays 3-4**
SUNDAY 3	Prologue. The visit to Nazareth (1)	Luke 1:1-4
		4:14-21
SUNDAY 4	The visit to Nazareth (2)	Luke 4:21-30

	The Galilean Ministry	Sundays 5-12
SUNDAY 5	*The call of the first apostles	Luke 5:1-11
SUNDAY 6	The sermon on the plain (1)	Luke 6:17, 20-26
SUNDAY 7	The sermon on the plain (2)	Luke 6:27-38
SUNDAY 8	The sermon on the plain (3)	Luke 6:39-45
SUNDAY 9	The cure of the centurion's servant	Luke 7:1-10
SUNDAY 10	*The widow of Naim	Luke 7:11-17
SUNDAY 11	*Jesus' feet anointed:	
	the sinful woman	Luke 7:36-8:3
SUNDAY 12	Peter's confession of faith	Luke 9:18-24

	The first part of the	
	'Travel Narrative':	**Sundays 13-23**
	The qualities Jesus demands of those who follow him	
SUNDAY 13	*The journey to Jerusalem begins	Luke 9:51-62
SUNDAY 14	*The mission of the seventy-two	Luke 10:1-12,17-20
SUNDAY 15	*The Good Samaritan	Luke 10:25-37
SUNDAY 16	*Martha and Mary	Luke 10:38-42
SUNDAY 17	*The importunate friend	Luke 11:1-13
SUNDAY 18	*The parable of the rich fool	Luke 12:13-21
SUNDAY 19	The need for vigilance	Luke 12:32-48
SUNDAY 20	'Not peace but division'	Luke 12:49-53
SUNDAY 21	Few will be saved	Luke 13:22-30
SUNDAY 22	True humility	Luke 14:1, 7-14
SUNDAY 23	The cost of discipleship	Luke 14:25-33

	The 'Gospel within the Gospel':	
	the message of pardon and reconciliation –	
	parables of God's mercy	**Sunday 24**
SUNDAY 24	*The lost coin, the lost sheep	
	and the prodigal son	Luke 15:1-32

	The second part of the	
	'Travel Narrative': the obstacles facing	
	those who follow Jesus	**Sundays 25-31**
SUNDAY 25	*The unjust steward	Luke 16:1-13
SUNDAY 26	*The rich man and Lazarus	Luke 16:19-31
SUNDAY 27	*A lesson on faith and dedication	Luke 17:5-10

SUNDAY 28	*The ten lepers	Luke 17:11-19
SUNDAY 29	*The unjust judge	Luke 18:1-8
SUNDAY 30	*The Pharisee and the tax collector	Luke 18:9-14
SUNDAY 31	*Zacchaeus	Luke 19:1-10
	The ministry in Jerusalem	**Sundays 32-33**
SUNDAY 32	The resurrection debated	Luke 20:27-38
SUNDAY 33	The signs announcing the end	Luke 21:5-19
	Christ the King: reconciliation	**Sunday 34**
SUNDAY 34	*The repentant thief	Luke 23:35-43

Appendix 3 _____

_____ *A Guide to Biblical Pronunciation*

This guide does not claim to be infallible. It is provided simply to help the reader with some general guidelines on pronunciation of the names of people and places in the Bible. These biblical names have been written phonetically, each syllable and vowel being given separately with its appropriate stress. There will be many readers whose mother tongue is not English. This list has been compiled not only to help those whose mother tongue is English, but also those who have to grapple both with the complexity of the English language and also have to find their way round some of the very strange looking biblical names and places. I hope that it will prove useful.

A brief explanation of the vowel sounds is given below, followed by a table of names with the syllable on which the stress falls printed in bold capital letters.

Vowels

Aa
- long a, (a̱) as in 'may', e.g. Ahaz
- short a, (a) as in 'bat', e.g. Abba, Amnon
- final a is pronounced 'ah', e.g. Cana, omega,
- ae is pronounced e, as in 'fee', e.g. Caesar, Alphaeus, but sometimes 'ay', e.g. Israel, Ishmael
- ai is pronounced i, as in 'bite', e.g. Jairus, Isaiah, but not always, e.g. Bethsaida (Beth-sa̱-i-da)
- ar is pronounced ah, as in final a, as in 'car', e.g. Hagar, Bartimaeus, or as long a, as in 'care', e.g. Pharoah, Aaron
- au is pronounced aw, as in 'law', e.g. Esau, Augustus

Ee

- long e, (e̱) as in 'fee', e.g. Belial, Eli, Mesach – occasionally 'ay', e.g. Puteoli
- short e, (e) as in 'get', e.g. Babel, Elisha
- ei is pronounced i, as in bite, e.g. Pleiades
- es is pronounced e̱, as in 'knees', in final syllable, like Artaxerxes, Boanerges
- eu is pronounced 'ew' as in 'hew', or 'you', e.g. Eutychus, Euphrates, Zeus. But Reuben is pronounced Rooben, and Reuel, Rooel

Ii

- long i, (i̱) pronounced 'eye' as in 'site', e.g. Shiloh, Philemon
- short i, (i) as in 'fit', e.g. Philippians, Agrippa
- final i is usually long, e.g. Haggai, Philippi, Eli; but sometimes short, e.g. Gehazi, Naomi

Oo

- long o, (o̱) as in 'dote', e.g. Obadiah, Ophir, Persepolis, Boaz
- short o, (o) as in 'hot', e.g. Enoch, Potifar, Omri
- oe is pronounced e, as in 'fee', e.g. Phoebe, Phoenician

Uu

- long u, (u̱) oo as in 'mood', e.g. Thummim, Talitha cumi, Methuselah
- short u, (u) oo as in 'soot', e.g. Habakkuk, Illyricum, Uzziah, but occasionally 'ew', e.g. Uriah, Chuza

Yy

- y as long i , as in 'why', e.g. Cyrene, Syro-Phoenician, Thyatira
- y as short i, as in 'jelly', e.g. Phrygia, Byblos, Ptolemy

Consonants

Cc

- as in English, hard before a, o and u, as in 'cap', 'cog', and 'cub', e.g. Cain, Colossus
- hard before consonants, e.g. Cleopas
- soft before e and i, as in 'ceiling', 'cipher', e.g. Cephas, Cilicia
- soft before ae and y, e.g. Caesarea, Cyrene. Exception: Cenchreae, initial c is hard

CHch
- is hard, as in 'chaos', e.g. Chemosh, Chloe, Chorazin. Exception: cherub, initial ch is soft, as in chary.

Gg
- is hard, as in 'got', e.g. Gaza, Gideon, Megiddo
- occasionally soft as in 'gender', e.g. Genesis, Niger, Phrygia

Jj
- soft g, as in 'jelly', e.g. Jesse, Judah, Elijah

PHph
- as in F, e.g. fridge, fright

SHsh
- as in shoe, shut

THth
- as in thing, thick, thirst

Stress

In order to indicate where the stress or accent falls in a name, the accented syllable is printed in bold capitals, for example Ma-ra-**NA**-tha.

Double vowels and consonants

To simplify further the phonetic pronunciation, where there are double consonants and vowels the one which would be mute anyway has been omitted.

Pronunciation of Biblical Names

Aaron	**A**-ron	Ahikar	a-**HI**-kar
Abana	a-**BA**-na	Ahitophel	a-**HI**-to-fel
Abba	**AB**-ba	Ai	**A**-i
Abednego	a-**BED**-ne-go	Akeldama	a-**KEL**-da-ma
Abel	**A**-bel	Alpha	**AL**-pha
Abel-Keramin	a-bel-ke-**RA**-min	Alphaeus	al-**PHAE**-us
Abel-Meholah	a-bel-me-**HO**-lah	Amalek	**A**-ma-lek
Abiathar	a-**BI**-a-thar	Amalekites	a-**MA**-le-kites
Abiel	a-bi-**EL**	Amaziah	a-ma-**ZI**-a
Abiezer	a-bi-**E**-zer	Amittai	a-mi-**TA**-i
Abijah	a-**BI**-jah	Amminadab	a-**MI**-na-dab
Abilene	a-bi-**LE**-ne	Ammonites	**A**-mo-nites
Abimelech	a-**BI**-me-lek	Amon	**A**-mon
Abinadab	a-**BI**-na-dab	Amorites	**A**-mo-rites
Abishai	a-bi-**SHA**-i	Amnon	**AM**-non
Abiud	a-**BI**-ud	Amos	**A**-mos
Abraham	**A**-bra-ham	Amoz	**A**-moz
Abiram	a-**BI**-ram	Ampliatus	am-pli-**A**-tus
Abishag	**A**-bi-shag	Anak	a-**NAK**
Absalom	**AB**-sa-lom	Ananias	a-na-**NI**-as
Aceldama	a-**CEL**-da-ma	Anastasia	a-na-**STA**-si-a
Achaia	a-**CHA**-i-a	Anathot(h)	**A**-na-thot(h)
Achbor	ach-**BOR**	Andronicus	an-**DRO**-ni-cus
Achim	**A**-chim	Antioch	**AN**-ti-och
Adar	**A**-dar	Antiochus	an-**TI**-o-chus
Adonijah	a-do-**NI**-jah	Antipas	**AN**-ti-pas
Adullam	a-**DU**-lam	Aphek	a-**PHEK**
Aeneas	ae-**NE**-as	Aphiah	a-**PHI**-ah
Aenon	**AE**-non	Apocalypse	a-**PO**-ca-lypse
Afam	**A**-fam	Apollos	a-**PO**-los
Agabus	**A**-ga-bus	Apollyon	a-**PO**-ly-on
Agag	**A**-gag	Aquila	**A**-qu-i-la
Agrippa	a-**GRI**-pa	Arabah	**A**-ra-bah
Ahab	**A**-hab	Aramaeans	a-ra-**MAE**-ans
Ahasuerus	a-ha-su-**E**-rus	Ararat	**A**-ra-rat
Ahaz	**A**-haz	Araunah	a-ra-**U**-nah
Ahaziah	a-ha-**ZI**-ah	Archelaus	ar-che-**LA**-us
Ahijah	a-**HI**-jah	Areopagite	a-re-**O**-pa-gite
Ahikam	a-**HI**-kam	Areopagus	a-re-**O**-pa-gus

Arimathaea	a-ri-ma-**THAE**-a	Bathsheba	bath-**SHE**-ba
Aristarchus	a-ri-**STAR**-chus	Becorath	be-**CO**-rath
Armageddon	ar-ma-**GE**-don	Beelzebub	be-**EL**-ze-bub
Aroer	a-**RO**-er	Beersheba	ber-**SHE**-ba
Artaxerxes	ar-tax-**ER**-xes	Belial	**BE**-li-al
Asa	**A**-sa	Belshazzar	bel-**SHA**-zar
Asaiah	A-**SA**-i-ah	Benaiah	be-**NA**-i-ah
Asaph	**A**-saph	Beor	be-**OR**
Ashdod	**ASH**-dod	Bernice	ber-**NI**-ce
Asher	**A**-sher	Bethpeor	beth-pe-**OR**
Ashkelon	**ASH**-ke-lon	Bethany	**BE**-tha-ny
Ashpenaz	**ASH**-pe-naz	Bethel	**BE**-thel
Ashtaroth	**ASH**-ta-roth	Bethmillo	beth-**MI**-lo
Asiel	**A**-si-el	Bethphage	**BETH**-pha-ge
Asmodeus	as-**MO**-de-us	Bethsaida	beth-**SA**-i-da
Assyria	as-**SY**-ria	Bethzatha	beth-**ZA**-tha
Astarte	as-**TAR**-te	Bethzur	beth-**ZUR**
Athaliah	a-**THA**-li-ah	Beulah	**BEU**-lah
Attalia	a-ta-**LI**-a	Bilhah	**BIL**-hah
Augustus	au-**GUS**-tus	Bithynia	bi-**THY**-ni-a
Azariah	a-za-**RI**-a	Boanerges	bo-an-**NER**-ges
Azarias	a-za-**RI**-as	Boaz	**BO**-az
Azor	**A**-zor	Bozrah	**BOZ**-rah
Azotus	a-**ZO**-tus	Buzi	**BU**-zi
Azzur	**A**-zur	Byblos	**BYB**-los
Baal	**BA**-al	Caesar	**CAE**-sar
Baal-Shalishah	**BA**-al-sha-**LI**-shah	Caesarea	cae-sa-**RE**-a
Baal-Zephon	**BA**-al-ze-**PHON**	C. Philippi	C. **PHI**-li-pi
Baasha	**BA**-sha	Caiaphas	**CA**-i-a-phas
Babel	**BA**-bel	Cain	**CA**-in
Babylon	**BA**-by-lon	Caleb	**CA**-leb
Bahurim	ba-**HU**-rim	Cana	**CA**-na
Balaam	**BA**-lam	Canaan	**CA**-na-n
Balak	**BA**-lak	Canaanite	**CA**-na-nite
Barabbas	ba-**RA**-bas	Candace	**CAN**-da-ce
Barak	**BA**-rak	Capernaum	ca-**PER**-na-um
Barnabas	**BAR**-na-bas	Caphtor	**CAPH**-tor
Barsabbas	bar-**SA**-bas	Cappadocia	ca-pa-**DO**-ci-a
Bartimaeus	bar-ti-**MAE**-us	Carchemish	**CAR**-che-mish
Baruch	**BA**-ruch	Cassia	**CA**-si-a
Bashan	**BA**-shan	Cenchreae	**CEN**-chre-ae

Cephas	**CE**-phas
Chaldeans	chal-**DAE**-ans
Chebar	**CHE**-bar
Chedorlaomer	che-dor-la-**O**-mer
Chemosh	**CHE**-mosh
Cherethites &	**CHE**-reth-ites
Pelethites	& **PE**-leth-ites
Cherith	**CHE**-rith
Cherubim	**CHE**-ru-bim
Chilion	**CHI**-li-on
Chislev	**CHIS**-lev
Chinnereth	**CHI**-ne-reth
Chloe	**CHLO**-e
Chorazin	cho-**RA**-zin
Chrysogonus	chry-**SO**-go-nus
Chusa	**CHU**-sa
Cilicia	ci-**LI**-ci-a
Cleophas	**CLE**-o-phas
Cletus	**CLE**-tus
Clopas	**CLO**-pas
Colossae	co-**LO**-sae
Colossians	co-**LO**-sians
	(co-**LOSH**-ans)
Corinthians	co-**RIN**-thi-ans
Cornelius	cor-**NE**-li-us
Cretans	**CRE**-tans
Crete	**CRETE**
Cushite	**CU**-shite
Cyprian	**CY**-pri-an
Cypriot	**CY**-pri-ot
Cyprus	**CY**-prus
Cyrene	cy-**RE**-ne
Cyrus	**CY**-rus
Dagon	**DA**-gon
Dalmanutha	dal-ma-**NU**-tha
Damaris	**DA**-ma-ris
Damascus	da-**MAS**-cus
Darius	**DA**-ri-us
Debir	de-**BIR**
Decapolis	de-**CA**-po-lis
Delilah	de-**LI**-lah

Derbe	**DER**-be
Deuteronomy	deu-te-**RO**-no-my
Didymus	**DI**-dy-mus
Dionysius	di-o-**NY**-si-us
Dothan	**DO**-than
Ebal	**E**-bal
Ebed-Melech	E-bed-**ME**-lech
Ebenezer	e-be-**NE**-zer
Ecbatana	ec-**BA**-ta-na
Ecclesiastes	ec-cle-si-**AS**-tes
Ecclesiasticus	ec-cle-si-**AS**-ti-cus
Edom	**E**-dom
El Shaddai	el-sha-**DA**-i
Elam	**E**-lam
Elamites	**E**-la-mites
Elath	**E**-lath
Eldad	**EL**-dad
Eleazar	e-le-**A**-zar
Eli	**E**-li
Eli, Eli lama sabachthani	
	E-li, **E**-li lama
	sa-bach-**TA**-ni
Eliab	e-**LI**-ab
Eliakim	e-**LI**-a-kim
Eliam	e-**LI**-am
Eliezer	e-li-**E**-zer
Elihu	e-**LI**-hu
Elijah	e-**LI**-jah
Elim	**E**-lim
Elimelech	e-**LI**-me-lech
Eliphaz	**E**-li-phaz
Elisha	e-**LI**-sha
Eliud	e-**LI**-ud
Elkanah	el-**KA**-nah
Elnathan	el-**NA**-than
Eloi	e-**LO**-i
Elymais	e-ly-**MA**-is
Emmanuel	e-**MA**-nu-el
Emmaus	e-**MA**-us
Engedi	en-**GE**-di
Enoch	**E**-noch

Epaenetus	e-pae-**NE**-tus	Gerasenes	**GE**-ra-s<u>e</u>nes
Epaphras	e-**PAPH**-ras	Gerizim	ge-ri-**ZIM**
Epaphroditus	e-**PAPH**-ro-**DI**-tus	Gethsemani	geth-**SE**-ma-ni
Ephah	**E**-phah	Gezer	**GE**-zer
Ephesians	e-**PHE**-si-ans	Gibeah	**GI**-be-ah
	(shans)	Gibeon	**GI**-be-on
Ephesus	**E**-phe-sus	Gibeonite	**GI**-be-o-n<u>i</u>te
Ephphatha	**EPH**-pha-tha	Gideon	**GI**-de-on
Ephraim	**E**-phra-im	Gihon	**GI**-hon
Ephraimite	**E**-phra-i-m<u>i</u>te	Gilboa	gil-**BO**-a
Ephrathah	**E**-phra-thah	Gilead	**GI**-le-ad
Ephron	**EPH**-r<u>o</u>n	Gilgal	**GIL**-gal
Epiphanes	e-**PI**-pha-nes	Girgashites	**GIR**-ga-sh<u>i</u>tes
Erastus	e-**RAS**-tus	Golan	**GO**-lan
Esau	**E**-sau	Golgotha	**GOL**-go-tha
Esdraelon	es-**DRAE**-lon	Goliath	go-**LI**-ath
Ethanim	**E**-tha-nim	Gomer	**GO**-mer
Ethiopia	<u>e</u>-thi-**O**-pi-a	Gomorrah	go-**MO**-ra
Euphrates	eu-**PHRA**-t<u>e</u>s	Goshen	**GO**-shen
Eutychus	**EU**-ty-chus	Gozan	**GO**-zan
Exodus	**EX**-o-dus		
Ezekiel	e-**ZE**-ki-el	Habakkuk	ha-**BA**-kuk
Ezra	**EZ**-ra	Habor	ha-**BOR**
		Hadad	**HA**-dad
Fortunatus	for-tu-**NA**-tus	Hades	**HA**-d<u>e</u>s
		Hagar	**HA**-gar
Gabbatha	**GA**-ba-tha	Haggai	ha-**GA**-i
Gadara	**GA**-da-ra	Hakeldama	ha-**KEL**-da-ma
Gadarenes	**GA**-da-r<u>e</u>-nes	Halah	**HA**-lah
Gaius	**GAI**-us	Haman	**HA**-man
Galatia	ga-**LA**-tia (sha)	Hananiah	ha-na-**NI**-ah
Galatians	ga-**LA**-tians (shans)	Hannah	**HA**-nah
Galilean	ga-li-**LE**-an	Haran	**HA**-ran
Gallio	**GA**-li-<u>o</u>	Havilah	**HA**-vi-lah
Gamaliel	ga-**MA**-li-el	Hazael	ha-**ZA**-el
Gaza	**GA**-za	Hazor	**HAZ**-or
Gehazi	ge-**HA**-zi	Heber	**HE**-ber
Gehenna	ge-**HE**-na	Hebrews	**HE**-brews
Genesis	**GE**-ne-sis	Hebron	**HE**-bron
Gennesaret	ge-**NE**-sa-ret	Helbon	**HEL**-bon
Gerar	**GE**-rar	Heliodorus	he-li-o-**DO**-rus
Gerasa	ge-**RA**-sa	Hellenists	**HE**-le-nists

Henoch	**HE**-noch	Jairus	**JAI**-rus
Hermes	**HER**-m<u>e</u>s	Japheth	**JA**-pheth
Herodians	he-**RO**-di-ans	Javan	**JA**-van
Herodias	he-**RO**-di-as	Jebusite	**JE**-bu-site
Hezekiah	he-ze-**KI**-ah	Jechoniah	je-cho-**NI**-ah
Hezron	**HEZ**-ron	Jeconiah	je-co-**NI**-ah
Hierapolis	hi-er-**A**-po-lis	Jeduthun	je-**DU**-thun
Hilkiah	hil-**KI**-ah	Jehoahaz	je-**HO**-a-haz
Hittite	**HI**-t<u>i</u>te	Jehoash	je-**HO**-ash
Hivites	**HI**-v<u>i</u>tes	Jehoiachin	je-**HO**-i-a-chin
Holofernes	ho-lo-**FER**-n<u>e</u>s	Jehoiada	je-**HO**-i-a-da
Hophni	**HOPH**-ni	Jehoiakim	je-**HO**-i-a-kim
Hor	**HOR**	Jehoram	je-**HO**-ram
Horeb	**HO**-reb	Jehoshaphat	je-**HO**-sha-fat
Hosea	h<u>o</u>-**SE**-a	Jehosheba	je-**HO**-sh<u>e</u>-ba
Hur	**HUR**	Jehozadak	je-**HO**-za-dak
		Jehu	**JE**-h<u>u</u>
Ichabod	**ICH**-a-bod	Jephthah	**JEPH**-thah
Iconium	<u>i</u>-**CO**-ni-um	Jeremiah	je-re-**MI**-ah
Iddo	**I**-d<u>o</u>	Jericho	**JE**-ri-ch<u>o</u>
Idumaea	i-du-**MAE**-a	Jeroboam	je-ro-**BO**-am
Illyricum	i-**LY**-ri-cum	Jeroham	je-**RO**-ham
Immanuel	i-**MA**-nu-el	Jerubaal	je-ru-**BAL**
Isaac	**I**-sac	Jesse	**JE**-s<u>e</u>
Isaiah	<u>i</u>-**SA**-i-ah	Jethro	**JETH**-r<u>o</u>
Iscariot	is-**CA**-ri-ot	Jezebel	**JE**-ze-bel
Ishbaal	**ISH**-b<u>a</u>l	Jezreel	**JEZ**-r<u>e</u>-el
Ishbosheth	ish-**BO**-sheth	Joab	**JO**-ab
Ishmael	**ISH**-m<u>a</u>-el	Joachim	**JO**-a-chim
Ishmaelite	**ISH**-m<u>a</u>-el-<u>i</u>te	Joakim	**JO**-a-kim
Israel	**IS**-r<u>a</u>-el	Joash	**JO**-ash
Israelite	**IS**-r<u>a</u>-el-<u>i</u>te	Job	**JOB**
Issachar	**I**-sa-char	Jochebed	**JO**-che-bed
Ithamar	**ITH**-a-mar	Joel	**JO**-el
Ituraea	i-tu-**RAE**-a	Jonah	**JO**-nah
		Joset	**JO**-set
Jabbok	**JA**-bok	Joshua	**JO**-shu-a
Jabesh-Gilead	**JA**-besh **GI**-le-ad	Josiah	jo-**SI**-ah
Jabin	**JA**-bin	Jotham	**JO**-tham
Jacob	**JA**-cob	Jubal	**JU**-bal
Jael	**JA**-el	Judaea	j<u>u</u>-**DAE**-a
Jair	**JA**-ir		

Judaean	ju-**DAE**-an	Machpela	mach-pe-la
Judah	**JU**-dah	Magdala	**MAG**-da-la
Judaism	**JU**-da-ism	Magdalene	**MAG**-da-lene
Junias	**JU**-ni-as	Magog	**MA**-gog
Justus	**JUS**-tus	Mahanaim	ma-ha-**NA**-im
		Maher-shalal-hash-baz	
Kadesh Barnea	**KA**-desh **BAR**-ne-a		**MA**-her-**SHA**-lal-
Kedar	**KE**-dar		**HASH**-baz
Kedesh-naphtali	**KE**-desh	Mahlon	**MAH**-lon
	NAPH-ta-li	Malachi	**MA**-la-chi
Kibroth-hattavah	**KI**-broth-	Malchiah	mal-**CHI**-ah
	ha-**TA**-vah	Malchus	**MAL**-chus
Kidron	**KID**-ron	Mamre	**MAM**-re
Kiriath-Arba	**KI**-ri-ath-**AR**-ba	Manaen	**MA**-na-en
Kirjath-jearim	**KIR**-jath-je-a-rim	Manasseh	ma-**NA**-seh
Kish	**KISH**	Manoah	ma-**NO**-ah
Kishon	**KI**-shon	Maranatha	ma-ra-**NA**-tha
		Marcelinus	mar-ce-**LI**-nus
Laban	**LA**-ban	Maresha	ma-**RE**-sha
Lachish	**LA**-chish	Massah	**MA**-sah
Lahai Roi	la-**HA**-i **RO**-i	Mattan	**MA**-tan
Lamech	**LA**-mech	Mattaniah	ma-ta-**NI**-ah
Laodicia	**LAO**-di-ce-a	Matthan	**MA**-than
Lazarus	**LA**-za-rus	Mattathias	ma-ta-**THI**-as
Leah	**LE**-ah	Matthias	ma-**THI**-as
Lebanon	**LE**-ba-non	Medad	**ME**-dad
Levi(tes)	**LE**-vi(tes)	Medes	**MEDES**
Leviathan	le-**VI**-a-than	Megiddo	me-**GI**-do
Leviticus	le-**VI**-ti-cus	Meholah	me-**HO**-lah
Lucius	**LU**-ci-us	Melchizedek	mel-**CHI**-ze-dek
Lud	**LUD**	Menahem	**ME**-na-hem
Luz	**LUZ**	Mene	**ME**-ne
Lycaonia	ly-ca-**O**-ni-a	Menelaus	me-ne-**LA**-us
Lydda	**LY**-da	Mephibosheth	me-**PHI**-bo-sheth
Lysanias	ly-**SA**-ni-as	Meribah	**ME**-ri-bah
Lysias	**LY**-si-as	Merodach-baladan	
Lystra	**LY**-stra		me-**RO**-dach-
			BA-la-dan
Maccabee	**MA**-ca-be	Meshach	**ME**-shach
Macedon	**MA**-ce-don	Mesopotamia	me-so-po-**TA**-mi-a
Macedonia	ma-se-**DO**-ni-a	Messiah	me-**SI**-ah
Machir	**MA**-chir		

Messianic	me-si-**A**-nic	Necho	**NE**-cho
Methuselah	me-**THU**-se-lah	Negeb	**NE**-geb
Micah	**MI**-cah	Nehemiah	ne-he-**MI**-ah
Micaiah	mi-**CA**-i-ah	Nehushtan	**NE**-hush-tan
Midian	**MI**-di-an	Nicanor	ni-**CA**-nor
Midianite	**MI**-di-a-nite	Nicodemus	ni-co-**DE**-mus
Milcom	mil-**COM**	Nicolaus	ni-co-**LA**-us
Miletus	mi-**LE**-tus	Nicopolis	ni-**CO**-po-lis
Minnith	**MI**-nith	Niger	**NI**-ger
Mishael	mi-**SHA**-el	Nimshi	**NIM**-shi
Mitylene	mi-ty-**LE**-ne	Nineveh	**NI**-ne-veh
Mizpah	**MIZ**-pah	Ninevites	**NI**-ne-vites
Moabite(ss)	**MO**-a-bite(ss)	Nisan	**NI**-san
Modein	**MO**-de-in	Noah	**NO**-ah
Mordecai	**MOR**-de-ca-i	Nun	**NUN**
Moreh	**MO**-reh		
Moresheth-gath	**MO**-resh-eth-**GATH**	Obadiah	o-ba-**DI**-ah
		Obed	**O**-bed
Moriah	mo-**RI**-ah	Og	**OG**
Moshach	**MO**-shech	Oholah	o-**HO**-lah
Mysia	**MY**-si-a	Oholibah	o-**HO**-li-bah
		Omega	**O**-me-ga
Naaman	**NA**-man	Omri	**OM**-ri
Nabal	**NA**-bal	Onan	**O**-nan
Naboth	**NA**-both	Onesimus	o-**NE**-si-mus
Nahor	**NA**-hor	Onesiphorus	o-ne-**SI**-pho-rus
Nahshon	nah-**SHON**	Onias	o-**NI**-as
Nahum	na-**HUM**	Ophir	**O**-phir
Nain	**NA**-in	Ophni	**O**-phni
Naomi	**NA**-o-mi	Ophrah	**O**-phrah
Naphtali	**NAPH**-ta-li	Orion	o-**RI**-on
Nathan	**NA**-than	Orpah	**OR**-pah
Nathanael	na-**THA**-na-el	Osnappar	os-**NA**-par
Nathaniel	na-**THA**-ni-el	Othniel	**OTH**-ni-el
Nazara	**NA**-za-ra		
Nazarene	**NA**-za-rene	Paddanaram	**PA**-dan-**A**-ram
Nazareth	**NA**-za-reth	Pamphylia	pam-**PHY**-li-a
Neapolis	ne-**A**-po-lis	Paphos	**PA**-phos
Nebat	**NE**-bat	Paran	**PA**-ran
Nebo	**NE**-bo	Parmenas	**PAR**-me-nas
Nebuchadnezzar	ne-bu-chad-**NE**-zar	Parsin	**PAR**-sin
		Parthians	**PAR**-thi-ans

Pashur	**PAS**-hur	Ptolemy	**PTO**-le-my
Pekah	**PE**-kah	Purim	**PU**-rim
Pekahiah	pe-ka-**HI**-ah	Put	**PUT**
Pelethites	**PE**-le-thites	Puteoli	pu-**TE**-o-li
Peniel	pe-**NI**-el		
Peninnah	pe-**NI**-nah	Quartus	**QUAR**-tus
Penuel	pe-**NU**-el	Quirinius	qui-**RI**-ni-us
Perez	**PE**-rez		
Perga	**PER**-ga	Raamses	**RAM**-ses
Pergamum	**PER**-ga-mum	Rabbah	**RA**-bah
Perizzites	**PE**-ri-zites	Rabbi	**RA**-bi
Perpetua	per-**PE**-tu-a	Rabbuni	ra-**BU**-ni
Persepolis	per-**SE**-po-lis	Raguel	**RA**-gu-el
Phanuel	**PHA**-nu-el	Rahab	**RA**-hab
Pharaoh	**PHA**-r(a)oh	Ramah	**RA**-mah
Pharisees	**PHA**-ri-ses	Ramathaim	ra-ma-**THA**-im
Pharpar	**PHAR**-par	Rameses	**RA**-me-ses
Philadelphia	phi-la-**DEL**-phi-a	Ramoth Gilead	**RA**-moth **GI**-le-ad
Philemon	phi-**LE**-mon	Raphael	**RA**-pha-el
Philetus	phi-**LE**-tus	Rebekah	re-**BE**-kah
Philippi	**PHI**-li-pi	Rechabites	**RE**-cha-bites
Philippians	phi-**LI**-pi-ans	Rehoboam	re-ho-**BO**-am
Philistia	phi-lis-**TI**-a	Remaliah	re-**MA**-li-ah
Philistines	**PHI**-lis-tines	Rephaim	re-**PHA**-im
Phinehas	**PHI**-ne-has	Rephidim	re-**PHI**-dim
Phoebe	**PHOE**-be	Reuben	**REU**-ben
Phoenicia	phoe-**NI**-ci-a (sha)	Reuel	**REU**-el
Phrygia	**PHRY**-gi-a	Rezin	**RE**-zin
Pihahiroth	pi-**HA**-hi-roth	Rhegium	**RHE**-gi-um
Pisgah	**PIS**-gah	Riblah	**RIB**-la
Pishon	**PI**-shon	Rosh	**ROSH**
Pisidia	pi-**SI**-di-a		
Pithom	**PI**-thom	Sabachthani	sa-bach-**TA**-ni
Pleiades	**PLEI**-a-des	Sabaeans	sa-**BAE**-ans
Pontius Pilate	**PON**-tius **PI**-late	Sadducees	**SAD**-u-ces
Potiphar	**PO**-ti-phar	Salamis	**SA**-la-mis
Praetorium	prae-**TO**-ri-um	Salem	**SA**-lem
Prisca	**PRIS**-ca	Salim	**SA**-lim
Prochorus	**PRO**-cho-rus	Salmon	**SAL**-mon
Procurator	**PRO**-cu-ra-tor	Salome	sa-**LO**-me
Ptolemais	pto-le-**MA**-is	Samaria	sa-**MA**-ri-a
		Samaritans	sa-**MA**-ri-tans

Samothrace	**SA**-mo-thrace	Shunem	**SHU**-nem
Samuel	**SA**-mu-el	Shur	**SHUR**
Sanballat	san-**BA**-lat	Sidon	**SI**-don
Sanhedrin	san-**HE**-drin	Sidonians	si-**DO**-ni-ans
Saphira	sa-**PHI**-ra	Sihon	**SI**-hon
Sarai	sa-**RA**-i	Silas	**SI**-las
Sardis	**SAR**-dis	Siloam	si-**LO**-am
Sceva	**SCE**-va	Silvanus	sil-**VA**-nus
Scythian	**SCY**-thi-an	Simeon	**SI**-me-on
Seba	**SE**-ba	Simon	**SI**-mon
Seir	**SEIR**	Sinai	**SI**-na-i
Seleucia	se-**LEU**-ci-a	Sinim	**SI**-nim
Seleucid	se-**LEU**-cid	Sinites	**SI**-nites
Sennacherib	se-**NA**-che-rib	Sisera	**SI**-se-ra
Sepharvaim	se-phar-**VA**-im	Smyrna	**SMYR**-na
Shaalim	**SHA**-a-lim	Sodom	**SO**-dom
Shaddai	sha-**DA**-i	Sodomites	**SO**-do-mites
Shadrach	**SHAD**-rach	Sosipater	so-**SI**-pa-ter
Shalisha	**SHA**-li-sha	Sosthenes	**SOS**-the-nes
Shallum	**SHA**-lum	Stachys	**STA**-chys
Shalmaneser	shal-ma-**NE**-ser	Stephanas	**STE**-pha-nas
Shammah	**SHA**-mah	Succoth	**SU**-coth
Shaphan	**SHA**-phan	Suph	**SUPH**
Shaphat	**SHA**-phat	Sychar	**SY**-char
Sharon	**SHA**-ron	Syene	**SY**-e-ne
Shealtiel	she-**AL**-ti-el	Synteche	**SYN**-te-che
Shear-jashub	**SHE**-ar-**JA**-shub	Syrophoenician	**SY**-ro-phoe-**NI**-ci-an
Sheba	**SHE**-ba		
Shebna	**SHEB**-na	Syrtis	**SYR**-tis
Shechem	**SHE**-chem	Taanach	**TA**-nach
Shemaiah	she-**MA**-i-ah	Tabeel	**TA**-be-el
Sheol	she-**OL**	Taberah	**TA**-be-rah
Shephat	**SHE**-phat	Tabitha	**TA**-bi-tha
Sheshbazzar	shesh-**BA**-zar	Talitha cumi	**TA**-li-tha **CU**-mi
Sheva	**SHE**-va	Tarshish	**TAR**-shish
Shibboleth	**SHI**-bo-leth	Tattenai	**TA**-te-na-i
Shiloh	**SHI**-loh	Tekel	**TE**-kel
Shimei	**SHI**-me-i	Tekoa	te-**KO**-a
Shinar	**SHI**-nar	Telabib	te-la-**BIB**
Shulammite	**SHU**-la-mite	Terah	**TE**-rah
Shunammites	**SHU**-na-**MITES**	Teraphim	**TE**-ra-phim

Tertius	**TER**-ti-us	Urim	**U**-rim
Tertullus	ter-**TU**-lus	Uzzah	**U**-zah
Tetrach	**TET**-rarch	Uzziah	u-**ZI**-ah
Thaddaeus	tha-**DAE**-us		
Thebes	**THE**-bes	Vashti	**VASH**-ti
Thebez	**THE**-bez	Xerxes	**XER**-xes
Theophilus	the-**O**-phi-lus		
Thessalonians	the-sa-**LO**-ni-ans	Yahweh	**YAH**-weh
Thessalonika	the-sa-**LO**-ni-ka		
Theudas	**THE**-u-das	Zacchaeus	za-**CHAE**-us
Thisbe	**THIS**-be	Zacharias	za-cha-**RI**-as
Thummim	**THU**-mim	Zadock	**ZA**-dok
Thyatira	thy-a-**TI**-ra	Zalmunna	zal-**MU**-na
Tiberias(us)	ti-**BE**-ri-as(us)	Zaphenath-peneah	
Timaeus	ti-**MAE**-us		**ZA**-phe-nath
Timon	**TI**-mon		pa-**NE**-ah
Tishbite	**TISH**-bite	Zarephath	**ZA**-re-phath
Titus	**TI**-tus	Zarethan	**ZA**-re-than
Tobias	to-**BI**-as	Zealot	ze-**A**-lot
Tobiel	to-**BI**-el	Zebedee	**ZE**-be-de
Tobijah	to-**BI**-jah	Zeboiim	ze-**BO**-im
Tobit	**TO**-bit	Zebulun	**ZE**-bu-lun
Tohu	**TO**-hu	Zechariah	ze-cha-**RI**-ah
Trachonitis	tra-cho-**NI**-tis	Zedekiah	ze-de-**KI**-ah
Trans-Euphrates	trans-eu-**PHRA**-tes	Zeeb	**ZE**-eb
Trans-Jordania	trans-jor-**DA**-ni-a	Zephaniah	ze-pha-**NI**-ah
Troas	**TRO**-as	Zerah	**ZE**-rah
Trophimus	**TRO**-phi-mus	Zeror	**ZE**-ror
Tryphon	**TRY**-phon	Zerubbabel	ze-**RU**-ba-bel
Tubal	**TU**-bal	Zeruiah	ze-ru-**I**-ah
Tubalcain	tu-bal-**CA**-in	Zeus	**ZE**-us
Tychicus	**TY**-chi-cus	Ziklag	**ZIK**-lag
Tyrannus	ty-**RA**-nus	Zimri	**ZIM**-ri
Tyre	**TYRE**	Zion	**ZI**-on
		Zipporah	**ZI**-po-rah
Ur	**UR**	Zoar	**ZO**-ar
Urbanus	ur-**BA**-nus	Zorah	**ZO**-rah
Uriah	u-**RI**-ah	Zuph	**ZUPH**
		Zuphite	**ZU**-phite

Bibliography

At Home with the Word. Sunday Scripture and Reflections – published annually by Liturgy Training Publications (LTP).

Documents of Vatican II – ed. Austin Flannery OP, Dominican Publications, 1975.

The General Instruction on the Roman Missal and *The General Instruction on the Lectionary* – both available in various editions.

God of Surprises – Gerard W Hughes, Darton, Longman & Todd, 1985.

Reading God's Word to Others – John Wijngaards, Mayhew-McCrimmon, 1981

The Right to Speak – Patsy Rodenburg, Methuen, 1982.

The Word among Us – *a daily approach to prayer and scripture* – monthly magazine; available from 6a Chapel Street, Cambridge CB4 1DY.

Workbooks for Lectors and Gospel Readers – published annually by LTP.

Further reading which may be helpful

Background to the Gospels – John Wijngaards, St Paul's Press.

Celebrating the Word – *A book for readers* – St Thomas More Centre.

The Daily Study Bible – William Barclay, St Andrew's Press, 1975.

The Dance of the Merrymakers – J. O'Hanlon, St Paul Publications, 1991.

Days of the Lord – *The Liturgical Year* (7 volumes), The Liturgical Press.

Eyes to See, Ears to Hear – D. Lonsdale SJ, Darton, Longman & Todd, 1990.

The Good News of Matthew, Mark and Luke's Year – Silvester O'Flynn OFM, Cathedral Books, The Columba Press, 1989.

How the Read the Old Testament and the New Testament – Etienne Charpentier, SCM Press, 1981.

The Inner Christ – John Main OSB, Darton, Longman & Todd, 1987.

The Liturgical Year – Adrian Nocent OSB (4 volumes), The Liturgical Press.

Paying Attention to God – William A Barry SJ, Ave Maria Press, 1990.

Acknowledgements _____

The publishers wish to express their gratitude to the following for permission to include copyright material in this publication:

Darton, Longman & Todd, 1 Spencer Court, 140-142 Wandsworth High Street, London SW18 4JJ, for the extract from *God of Surprises* by Gerard Hughes, published and © copyright 1985 Darton, Longman & Todd.

Dominican Publications, 42 Parnell Square, Dublin 1, for the extracts from *Vatican II: Conciliar and Post-conciliar Documents*, edited by Austin Flannery, OP, © copyright 1975 Dominican Publications.

International Commission on English in the Liturgy, 1522 K Street NW, Suite 1000, Washington, DC 20005-1202, USA, for excerpts from the English translation of the Introduction from the *Lectionary for Mass* © 1981 International Committee on English in the Liturgy, Inc. All rights reserved.

McCrimmon Publishing Co, 10-12 High Street, Great Wakering, Southend-on-Sea, Essex, SS3 0EQ, for the extract from *Reading God's Word to Others* by John Wijngaards, © copyright McCrimmons 1981.

Mgr Michael Smith for the extracts 'Commissioning of Parish Readers', taken from *Services for use in the Archdiocese of Southwark*, edited by Tom Coyle and Mgr Michael Smith, and the 'Rite of Renewal of Commitment of Parish Readers', © copyright 1984 Southwark Liturgy Commission.

Bible quotations are taken from the following sources:

The *Revised Standard Version*, © 1946, 1952 and 1971, The Division of Christian Education and the National Council of the Church of Christ in the USA.

The *New Jerusalem Bible*, © copyright 1985 Darton, Longman & Todd.

The *New English Bible*, © copyright 1961, 1970, Oxford and Cambridge University Presses.

Every effort has been made to trace the owners of copyright material and we hope that no copyright has been infringed. Pardon is sought and apology made if the contrary be the case, and a correction will be made in any reprint of this book.